USA AND ITS ECONOMIC FUTURE

A TWENTIETH CENTURY FUND SURVEY

USA

and Its Economic Future

by
ARNOLD B. BARACH

graphics by
RUDOLF MODLEY

THE MACMILLAN COMPANY · NEW YORK

This book is based on

AMERICA'S NEEDS AND RESOURCES: A NEW SURVEY

by J. FREDERIC DEWHURST *and associates*

Statistics brought up to date
by MILTON KELENSON
under the direction of J. FREDERIC DEWHURST

WHERE DOES THE AMERICAN ECONOMIC SYSTEM *stand today—and where is it likely to stand tomorrow? Not only Americans, but persons throughout the world, are interested in the answers.*

In bringing forward relevant facts, presented in simply written style and reinforced by graphic illustrations, this book follows two widely used predecessors, U.S.A.: MEASURE OF A NATION *(1949) and* U.S.A. IN NEW DIMENSIONS *(1957). In the earlier versions, the material was derived directly from the Twentieth Century Fund's two large-scale, pioneering studies of* AMERICA'S NEEDS AND RESOURCES *(1947 and 1955), both directed by J. Frederic Dewhurst.*

Recognizing the need for more current material, the Fund's Board of Trustees authorized a somewhat different approach for the present book. Instead of doing a full-scale new study of America's needs and resources, updated statistics and other materials were assembled directly for this book. This resulted in large savings of time of preparation and more current factual findings.

Two innovations will be noted. First, there is an annotated, statistical appendix that gives much more extensive factual information. The hope is that this may enhance the usefulness of U.S.A. AND ITS ECONOMIC FUTURE *for businessmen, public officials, students, and interested persons generally. The second innovation is that the book is being issued at the same time as a similar presentation of* THE NEW EUROPE AND ITS ECONOMIC FUTURE. *The factual material for both books was assembled under the general supervision of Dr. Dewhurst, and taken together the books portray the economic bases upon which the two chief elements in the North Atlantic region may seek to work out meaningful relationships with each other.*

The text of the present book was written by Arnold B. Barach, Senior Editor of CHANGING TIMES, *the Kiplinger magazine, and the Fund pays tribute to the professional skill and dedicated interest that he brought to the task. As with the two predecessor books, the graphics were provided by Rudolf Modley, a distinguished pioneer in this form of presentation. The individual drawings were done by Stephen Kraft, and the design of the book, the typography, and page layouts were done by Hubert Leckie. The cover was designed by Charles Forberg. Mrs. Frances Klafter, of the Fund's Washington staff, served with great effectiveness as chief editor and coordinator of the project; Milton Kelenson did the major work of updating statistics and assembling new material; and Thomas R. Carskadon, Associate Director, and Louise Field, Research Associate of the Fund, kept in close touch with the project from the beginning. To all of these, to Dr. Dewhurst, to The Macmillan Company, the publisher with which once again we are pleased to be associated, the Fund extends its grateful thanks.*

August Heckscher, *Director*
THE TWENTIETH CENTURY FUND

CONTENTS

chapter

CHAPTER I

America in Today's World

PROSPEROUS, STRONG, CHALLENGED: these words describe the America of the 1960s. Her people enjoy a higher standard of living than ever before. Her agriculture and industry reflect the riches of America's technology, resources, and manpower. Millions of the world's people look to her for leadership, while others challenge her ability to maintain economic preeminence in an era of change.

America in the sixties How well prepared is America to cope with the demands of the sixties and the seventies to come? Can the nation's present prosperity be sustained? Can its rate of economic growth be increased? Will the country retain its leadership as an economic power? Can it develop a working relationship with the other nations on both sides of the North Atlantic that will be beneficial to all?

To answer these questions, one needs an accurate measure of the American economy as it functions today and a sound appraisal of where it will be tomorrow.

The Twentieth Century Fund undertook such a measure of America in the 1950s and published its conclusions in 1955 in a report called *America's Needs and Resources: A New Survey*. This volume is based in part on that report, but with the findings, conclusions, and projections brought up to date.

Measure of a nation In the early 1960s, America stood at the peak of her economic strength. She led the world in total production of goods and services and in output per person. Almost 70 million people were at work. The average

1

family income was more than $7,100 a year. New houses were being built at the rate of about 1.5 million annually. More than 7 million new automobiles came off the assembly lines each year. From the nation's factories poured an incredible number of TV sets and air-conditioning units, automatic washers and refrigerators, synthetic fabrics and processed foods. America's storehouse of consumer goods of high quality seemed inexhaustible.

GNP PER PERSON, 1960

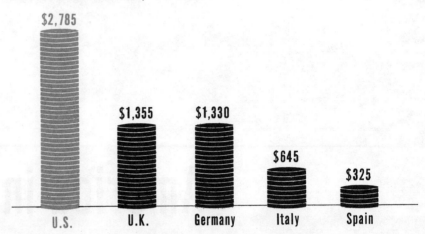

$2,785	$1,355	$1,330	$645	$325
U.S.	U.K.	Germany	Italy	Spain

This achievement seems even more remarkable when it is recalled that less than 20 years earlier the United States had emerged from its most devastating and exhausting war, a war preceded by almost 10 years of the worst depression in American history.

War and aftermath During the war years, the nation's economy had attained hitherto unprecedented levels. Output of agricultural products, oil, steel, aluminum, coal, lumber, cement, and manufactured goods had outstripped the boom era of the 1920s. With the end of the war came a flood of cars, refrigerators, air conditioners, radios, washing machines, and other consumer goods to fill the vacuum left by the years when production for war had almost halted production of consumer durable goods.

Underpinnings for the future It was in these years and in the early 1950s—when the Korean War pushed industrial activity to new levels—that the foundations were laid for the growth of the 1960s.

A multitude of new materials and products appeared: synthetic rubber and fibers, plastics, miracle drugs, fungicides and insecticides, synthetic detergents, new and improved building materials, television sets, home freezers, air conditioners—to mention but a few. The application of atomic energy to peaceful uses loomed as one of the most promising developments of the period. Brilliant discoveries in electronics, biochemistry, physics, and the other sciences established the groundwork for America's participation in the space age.

Baby boom The country's population, which had grown at only about 900,000 a year in the 1930s, expanded at a rate of close to 3 million a year in the mid-1950s, as the postwar "baby boom" continued. About a million new families were setting up housekeeping each year in the fifties.

2

Incomes rose. Average hourly earnings of factory workers, for example, were $1.02 in 1945. By mid-1963 they had reached a level of $2.45 an hour. Inflation had reduced the value of the dollar by 41 cents, but, even so, the increase in the factory worker's real earnings was 40 per cent.

Thousands of new businesses were established and older businesses expanded. As a result, many new jobs were created.

In addition to millions of new dwellings, builders were busy erecting schools, stores, churches, hospitals, factories, power plants, office buildings. And a new 41,000-mile superhighway network was started.

These were but a few of America's dimensions for the 1960s.

GNP almost $600 billion In 1953, the nation's gross national product (GNP)—the value of all goods and services it produces—was $365 billion. Ten years later, it had reached $585 billion. Americans were proud of the country's productive achievement.

It was an achievement to which others in the world aspired. The United States, with hardly more than 6 per cent of the world's population, less than 7 per cent of its land area, and about the same proportion of its natural resources, produces almost a third of the world's oil, a fourth of its steel, almost half of its motor vehicles.

Success secret: high productivity How does America do it? There are many answers to this question. The most important is the nation's rising productivity—its ability to produce an increasing quantity of goods and services per unit of manpower. A century ago the average factory worker put in over 60 hours a week. The work week of today's factory worker averages 40 hours. But today, output per worker (in terms of national income in constant dollars) is more than six times that of 1850.

The country's climate, its natural resources, and its fertile land, though great endowments, do not alone account for this ability to produce far more per worker than any other nation in the world. More than anything else, America's economic accomplishments are the result of her lavish use of the fruits of technology: machines, power, new materials, industrial techniques, and scientific and industrial research.

CHANGES IN PRODUCTIVITY, 1850-1975

By 1975 each worker will be producing almost 12 times as much as the worker of 1850.

1850 ▮

1900 ▮▮

1950 ▮▮▮▮▮

1960 ▮▮▮▮▮▮

1975 ▮▮▮▮▮▮▮▮▮▮▮

Each symbol represents 50 cents, at 1960 prices, of national income per man-hour of private employment.

3

U.S. POSITION IN THE WORLD, EARLY 1960s

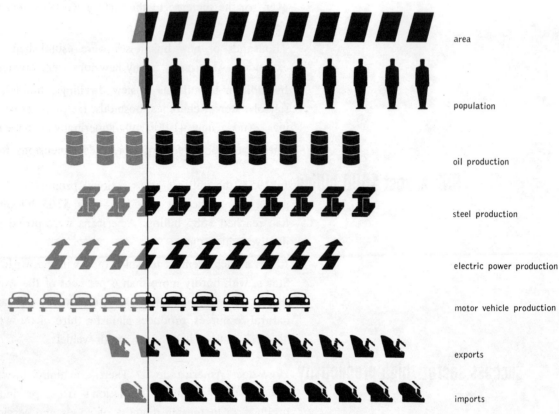

United States | Rest of World

area

population

oil production

steel production

electric power production

motor vehicle production

exports

imports

Each symbol represents 10 per cent of world total.

Despite its achievements, the America of the 1960s has by no means solved all its problems.

There is unemployment. In the early 1960s about 5.5 per cent of the nation's total labor force was out of work. This was not too far from what the Twentieth Century Fund's 1955 study had predicted as likely, based on the experience of the last "normal" boom years of the 1920s, when average unemployment was about 5 per cent.

There is poverty. About 14 million families, 30 per cent of all families in the United States, have incomes of less than $4,000 a year.

There are slums. Despite the accomplishments of redevelopment programs, America's cities and towns still have millions of substandard homes. The 1960 Housing Census reports that one out of five housing units, exclusive of those lacking some plumbing facilities, is dilapidated or deteriorating.

Problems to be solved There are community problems. Schools and school personnel, water resources, public services, recreational facilities have not kept pace with the growing population and thus the growing needs, now and for the future.

There is dissatisfaction with economic growth. Many industries fail to operate at their full capacity. The economy's growth rate (rate of growth in total GNP in constant prices) from 1957 to 1962 was only about 2.9 per cent a year, compared with 3.8 per cent from 1947 to 1957. Great difficulties are experienced in absorbing the 700,000 young people who leave school and look for jobs each year. Many of these young job-seekers have not finished high school and are thus poorly equipped to find employment in a nation which puts a premium on education and skills. Coupled with this is the problem of retraining older workers whose skills are no longer needed in an age of growing automation.

They can be overcome These are but a few of the problems for which serious-minded Americans are seeking solutions in the 1960s. They are not insurmountable. The American resourcefulness in coping with difficulties and in overcoming obstacles has given the American economic system the dynamic quality which characterized it in the past and which will strengthen it in the future.

AMERICA LOOKS AHEAD

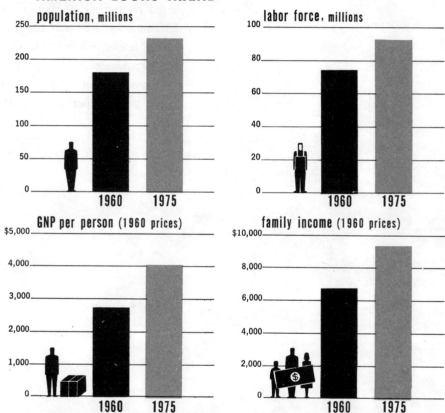

Even at its present moderate rate of growth, the nation's prospects are promising. Present trends indicate that in 1975 the nation will be bigger, richer, and far more productive than it is today. Population will be approximately 235 million. There will be about 87 million people in civilian jobs and 3 million in the armed forces. But, even with measures being taken to reduce unemployment, such as retraining programs for people displaced by automation and for other reasons, there is little hope that fewer than 3.5 million people—or 4 per cent of the labor force—will be unemployed.

The promise of 1975 Assuming that productivity increases year by year at about the same rate as today, the average worker in 1975 will be producing 53 per cent more goods and services than in 1962. Put another way, the average value of his hourly output, expressed in 1960 prices, will be $5.80 compared to $3.80 in 1962.

The GNP will also grow impressively. If the work week remains unchanged, and if employment and productivity reach anticipated levels, by 1975 the nation's output of goods and services could reach $955 billion (in 1960 prices).

Living standards will rise with this growing national wealth. There will be many millions more families with annual incomes of $10,000 and over. Average family income is expected to be $9,525 a year (in 1960 prices).

A tradition and a responsibility

There may be those who are dubious of the nation's ability to attain these levels. But such growth is in the nation's tradition. In 1960, for example, output was 35 times that of 1850, but the 1960 population was only 8 times that of 1850.

In that period, the secret of growth was the mastery of the machine and the harnessing of steam and electric power. Tomorrow's progress will be based on further developments in technology and science, which will determine in large part the future dimensions of America and its position of leadership in the world. Based on the record of her past growth and her prospects for the future, the United States should continue in the front ranks of the nations of the North Atlantic, contributing greatly to her own prosperity and to the prosperity of her neighbors and of the world.

6

CHAPTER II

Expanding Population

PEOPLE MAKE THE NATION. They give it its knowledge and its skills, its talents and its strength. So it is important to know how America's population has grown and changed and how it looked as the nation moved into the sixties.

The population of the United States quadrupled in the first half of the nineteenth century. It more than tripled in the second half. It doubled again in the first half of this century. By 1950, there were nearly seven times as many Americans as there had been 100 years earlier.

In 10 years, 28 million people In the 1950s an unprecedented 28 million people were added to the population, and at the beginning of the 1960s the country was growing at the record rate of nearly 3 million persons a year.

Never before had so many people been added to the population in so short a time—not even at the peak of the immigration flood just before World War I, when 1 million persons a year entered the United States.

For three quarters of a century immigrants had been streaming in from their European homelands—Germany and Ireland, Scandinavia and Austria-Hungary, Italy and Russia, Greece and the Balkan countries. Together with the British, the French and the Spaniards, who had come earlier, these newcomers produced a lasting bond between America and Europe—particularly Western Europe.

Changing social and economic conditions have a marked effect on population trends.

In the depression years of the 1930s, for example, there was a slowing

7

POPULATION GROWTH, 1800-1975

By 1975 population is expected to reach 235 million, compared with the 1960 Census count of 179 million.

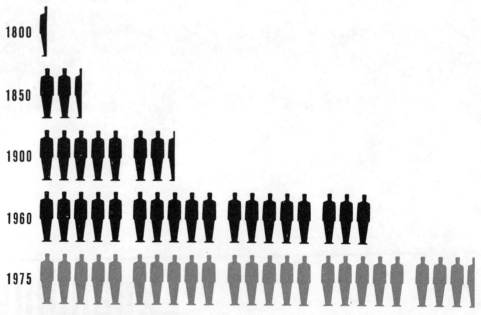

Each symbol represents 10 million persons.

of the population growth. Immigration practically ceased. Birth rates fell, as fewer couples could afford to marry and have children.

Wedding bells ring This was the situation on the eve of World War II, when couples who had been delaying weddings decided to wait no longer. By 1942 the marriage rate had reached a new high—115 marriages per 1,000 women aged 17 to 29. The end of the war caused another jump in the marriage rate. By 1946, it had risen to 148 per 1,000, for a record 2.3 million weddings. From 1946 to 1950, some 9 million couples took the marriage vows.

MARRIAGE RATES

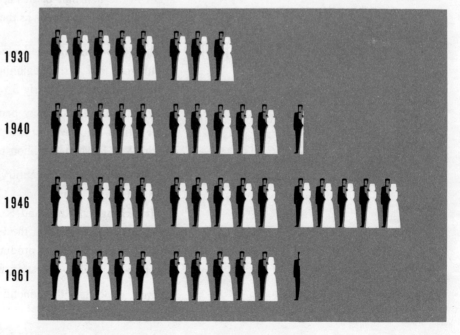

Each symbol represents 10 marriages per 1,000 women aged 17-29.

By the 1950s, the marriage rate had slowed somewhat, but was still at a high level. Each year, right up to 1962, there was an average of about one and a half million weddings.

Brides of 1949 to 1962—half of them 20 or under—were nearly 2 years younger than their grandmothers or great grandmothers had been when they married in 1890. Grooms—half of them under 23—were three and a half years younger than their grandfathers or great grandfathers had been when they got married. Curiously enough, the "marrying age" was returning to what it had been in Colonial times.

In these years, the base was established for the phenomenal population increase that the country has been experiencing and will continue to experience. In 1940, 2.6 million babies were born. But in 1957, an all-time record 4.3 million babies arrived. Births in the 1950s totaled nearly 41 million. This was the much-vaunted "baby boom" and its results quickly became visible in the country's playgrounds, nursery schools, and elementary schools.

Birth rate up — death rate down

As the birth rate rose, the death rate continued to fall—as it had almost uninterruptedly since the beginning of the century. In 1900, the death rate was 17.2 out of every 1,000 Americans. By 1961, it was down to 9.3 per 1,000, or about half of what it had been 61 years earlier. Conquest of disease, particularly diseases of infants and children, had produced this change. Whereas a male child born in 1900 could expect to live to 46, one born in 1960 had a life expectancy of 67. For females, the gain has been even greater, from a life expectancy of 48 in 1900 to 73 in 1960.

EXCESS OF BIRTHS OVER DEATHS, 1900-1960

1900

1920

1940

1950

1960

Each symbol represents 2 births (or deaths) per 1,000 population.

One other development contributed to the soaring population curve. Congress lowered the immigration barriers for a few years after World War II to make room for displaced eastern Europeans who did not choose to return to their homelands. In addition, large numbers of immigrants came to the United States from Canada and other nations in the American hemisphere. A total of nearly 3 million immigrants—the largest number since the 1920s—settled in the United States in the 1950s.

Here is how America's population had changed by 1960:

● In 1940, one out of four Americans was under 15 years of age. In 1960, about one out of three was this young. The nation was definitely getting younger.

● Those in the 20-to-29-year age bracket constituted 16 per cent of the total population in 1950, 12 per cent in 1960.

● There were 3 million more 30-to-44-year-olds in 1960 than in 1950, but because population was increasing so fast they made up a slightly smaller percentage (20.5 per cent in 1960, rather than the 21.9 per cent of 1950).

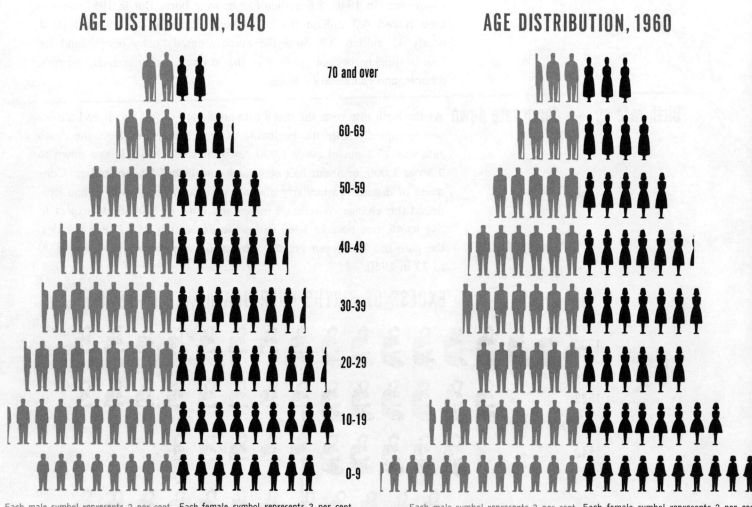

AGE DISTRIBUTION, 1940

AGE DISTRIBUTION, 1960

70 and over

60-69

50-59

40-49

30-39

20-29

10-19

0-9

Each male symbol represents 2 per cent of total male population. Each female symbol represents 2 per cent of total female population.

Each male symbol represents 2 per cent of total male population. Each female symbol represents 2 per cen of total female population.

● Finally, because of increasing longevity and the falling death rate, the number of persons over 65 reached an all-time high of 16 million in 1960—1 out of every 11 Americans. Never before had the country had so many "senior citizens," and never before had they constituted so large a percentage of the total population.

As these changes were occurring, there were other trends. The nation's Negro population rose rapidly, a result of better health care and improving economic conditions. By 1961, there were over 19 million Negroes in the United States, compared to 15 million 10 years earlier. Together with other nonwhites, they now accounted for between 11 and 12 of every 100 Americans, compared with about 10 in 1930 and 1940.

A women's world At midcentury, a historic shift took place in America's population: for the first time, women outnumbered the men. In 1950, there were 993 men for every 1,000 women. By 1960, there were only 978 men for every 1,000 women. By 1970, it is estimated that there will be still fewer—972 men for every 1,000 women.

Luckily, it is in the marrying ages (up to 25) that young men outnumber the girls. After that, because women live longer, there are more females than males. After 65, there are almost 10 women for every 8 men.

Early marriages, combined with prosperous economic conditions, have caused a rapid rise in the formation of new households. Including single persons living alone, there were 55 million separate households in the country in 1962. Married couples under 45 generally had 2 or 3 children, not much of an increase from a decade earlier.

One unhappy development marred this domestic picture. By 1960 more than one out of four marriages was ending in the divorce courts, compared with about one out of six in 1940. There are more people marrying in haste and repenting at leisure than there were in pre–World War II days.

THE FLIGHT FROM THE FARM

Today, only 1 of every 14 Americans is a farm dweller. In 1920 almost one of every three persons lived on a farm.

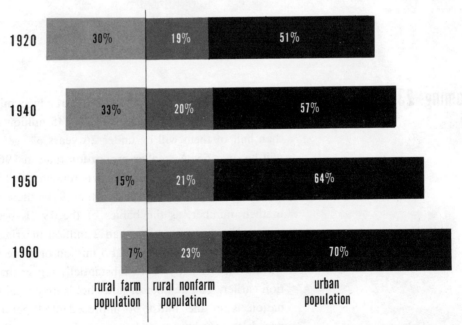

	rural farm population	rural nonfarm population	urban population
1920	30%	19%	51%
1940	33%	20%	57%
1950	15%	21%	64%
1960	7%	23%	70%

A new definition of "urban" in 1960 gives somewhat greater emphasis to the shift. Data for 1950 and 1960 are based on the new definition.
Data are for continental United States only.

Suburban life Where does this expanding population like to live? Between 60 and 70 per cent of all Americans now live in urban areas. These city dwellers are divided about equally between the suburbs and the central cities.

For many years families have been moving out of the city and into the suburbs, but there are signs of disenchantment with suburban living. The first indication of movement back to the city can be seen.

There have also been regional migrations—to the West, the Southwest, and the Southeast (mainly Florida). Much of this movement has been that of retired people seeking pleasant climates.

Dating back to 1920, there has been a consistent and almost uninterrupted flight from the farm. By 1962, only 14.3 million people were left on the farms, in contrast to about 32 million 40 years earlier.

GEOGRAPHIC POPULATION SHIFTS, 1950-1960

The Southwest and Florida are growing fastest . . .

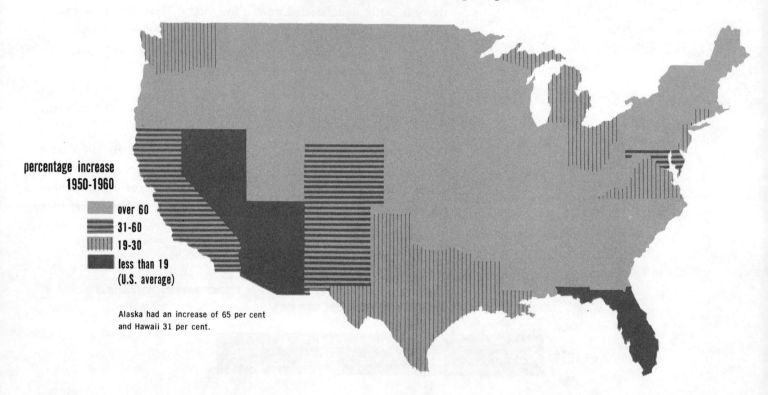

percentage increase
1950-1960

over 60
31-60
19-30
less than 19
(U.S. average)

Alaska had an increase of 65 per cent
and Hawaii 31 per cent.

Coming: 235 million people

The population picture of 1975 is already coming into focus. At the present rate of growth, there will be 235 million Americans then. More than half of them will be under 26 years of age. More than 22 million will be over 65. A smaller proportion than in 1960 will be in the working ages—between 15 and 64. Whereas in the 1960s there was a drop of those in the marrying ages, in the 1970s there will be a dramatic rise in their number, as the babies of the 1950s become young men and women. As a result, more than 2 million marriages can be expected in 1975. Births are likely to total 5 million or more in that year, and there will be another baby boom substantially bigger than the one of a generation earlier. The number of households may total 68 million. Today, the nation is in the midst of unprecedented population growth—but a decade or so from now today's records will be eclipsed.

CHAPTER III

Americans at Work

AMERICANS ARE, above all, a busy, enterprising people, working at an endless variety of jobs, producing what the nation needs.

A busy, industrious people They man production lines, run railroads, staff hospitals, operate stores, teach school, mine the earth, cultivate farms, work in research laboratories, administer government offices, and perform the other tasks vital to a thriving and expanding economy.

More than one out of every three Americans—a total of about 68 million—were employed in civilian jobs in 1962, more than ever before in war or peace.

Not all the employed people were on someone else's payroll. About one out of eight was self-employed—his own boss. The self-employed were businessmen, farmers, doctors, lawyers, merchants, repairmen, and other independent workers.

Unemployment blight While 68 million were employed in 1962, the total number in the labor force was about 75 million. Of these, nearly 3 million were in the armed forces. The remainder—about 4 million, or almost 5.6 per cent of the civilian labor force—were, for one reason or another, unemployed. They posed one of the most serious domestic problems confronting the nation and its government.

Changing labor force This labor force was different from that of even a generation earlier. It had more women in it, for one thing. It contained a higher proportion of workers 45 and over. It also included smaller proportions of

THE CHANGING LABOR FORCE

In less than 100 years, farmers dropped from 50 per cent of the labor force to less than 10 per cent.

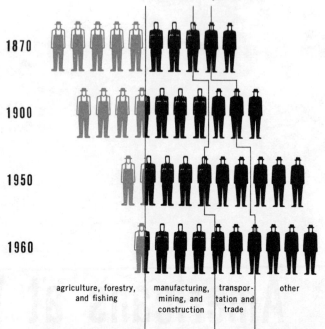

agriculture, forestry, and fishing   manufacturing, mining, and construction   transportation and trade   other

Each symbol represents 10 per cent of the labor force.

workers on the nation's farms and in its industrial plants.

Many of the changes had been under way for over half a century—the gradual influx of women into the labor force, for instance, and the shift out of agriculture to other occupations. But these trends had been speeded up by the technological and social changes brought on by World War II.

Looking back, certain definite trends come into focus:

● Child labor, less than 50 years ago one of the major social issues of the day, is no longer a problem.

The disappearing farm worker ● Farming has become less and less significant in the total employment picture. As recently as 1940, 17 out of every 100 workers depended on agriculture for their jobs. But in 1962, only about 7 out of 100 worked on farms—a result of technological and scientific advances in agriculture. Thus, American agriculture has become so productive that 1 farm worker today supplies not only himself and 27 other Americans with the farm products they need—he produces a surplus for export.

Women leave home ● Women make up a larger proportion of the labor force than ever before. In 1920, one out of five in the labor force was a woman; in 1940, one out of four; in 1960, one out of three. This rapid gain in female employment is due in part to the need or urge to supplement family income, in part to women's desire to escape the boredom of housework. Modern appliances, convenience foods, and other labor savers leave many housewives feeling they are wasting much of their talent and ability.

Ascendancy of the white collar ● White-collar workers—the office workers, store clerks, computer operators, doctors, lawyers, teachers—now outnumber blue-collar work-

14

ers—the machine operators, miners, construction workers. There was a 50 per cent increase in white-collar workers between 1947 and 1962. By 1962, 44 out of every 100 working people were in white-collar jobs, compared to only 36 out of every 100 working people engaged in blue-collar occupations. People working on farms—both farm owners and farm workers of various kinds—made up 7 per cent of the employed, while persons engaged in various kinds of service occupations accounted for the remaining 13 per cent.

Expanding services • Industries which do not produce goods—mined, manufactured, or agricultural—are called "service industries." These industries employ white- and blue-collar workers, and also people in strictly service occupations, such as maids, firemen, bartenders, barbers, waiters, etc. Service industries include barbershops, stores, insurance and real-estate firms, banks, travel agencies, government offices, transportation facilities, public utilities, delivery services, laundries, dry-cleaning shops, repair shops, and dozens of other places which provide a wide range of services to meet the needs of others. They have grown greatly in importance since World War II in terms of the proportion of the labor force which they employ, which increased from about 49 per cent in 1947 to about 58 per cent in 1962.

The labor force is older As these changes were taking place, the labor force was getting older. In 1890, for example, half the male workers in the country were under 33, but by 1960 the dividing age was 39. For women workers, this upward trend in age has been much sharper; half were under 24 in 1890, but in 1960 the dividing age was 40. The trend toward an older labor force has been due to a decline in child labor and farming; an extension of school years, keeping teen-agers out of the job market longer; and to the fact that there are more people 45 and over than there used to be.

WHO IS IN THE LABOR FORCE ?

In 1962, there were 75 million men and women at work, in the armed forces, or looking for jobs.

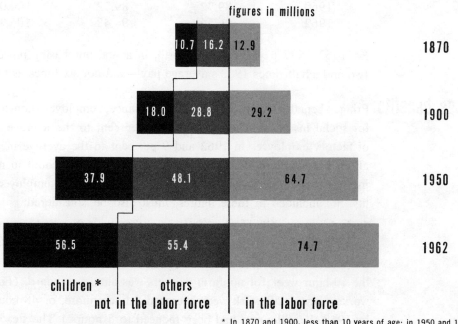

figures in millions

10.7	16.2	12.9	1870
18.0	28.8	29.2	1900
37.9	48.1	64.7	1950
56.5	55.4	74.7	1962

children * | others | in the labor force
not in the labor force

* In 1870 and 1900, less than 10 years of age; in 1950 and 1962, less than 14 years of age.

A smaller percentage of workers over 65 are staying on their jobs in the 1960s. The main reasons are the government social security program, the rapid spread of private pension plans, and the growing practice of making retirement compulsory by age 65.

Good pay Young or old, white-collar or blue-collar, the worker of the sixties was better off financially and in other ways than most of his predecessors.

FACTORY WORKER'S WEEKLY PAY
in 1960 dollars

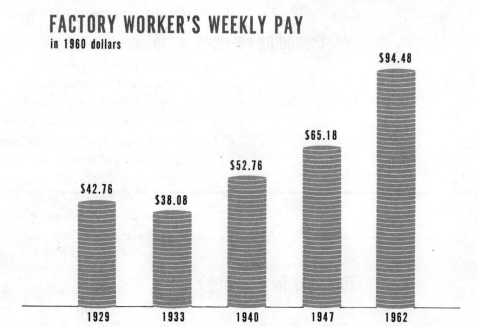

The average pay in manufacturing in 1962, for instance, was $97 a week—double the 1947 average and nearly six times as much as in the depression year of 1933. However, inflation had milked the dollar of much of its purchasing power in the years since World War II, as the following figures show:

year	actual pay	its value in 1960 dollars	index: 1960=100
1933	$16.65	$38.08	42.4
1947	49.17	65.18	72.6
1960	89.72	89.72	100.0
1962	96.56	94.48	105.3

So, 1962's $97 pay check was worth, in actual purchasing power, only two and a half times 1933's average pay—and not six times as much.

Fringe benefits Fringe benefits—pensions, health insurance, employer contributions for social insurance—added about 11 per cent to the average income of factory employees in 1962 and 9 per cent to the average income of all civilian workers. Thus, they must be taken into account in measuring pay scales. Paid vacations, holiday pay, and other employee benefits, not included in these figures, must also be considered.

Today's workers also have more leisure time than their fathers and their grandfathers had. Between 1850 and 1950, the average work week dropped about 3 hours each decade—or 30 hours total. By midcentury, the 40-hour week for nonfarm workers was almost standard. (For farm workers, the 1950 work week averaged 8 hours more, or 48 hours, but by 1962 the difference had been reduced to 5 hours.) The steady drop in the work week came almost to a halt between 1950 and 1960—but this was apparently only a pause in the long-term trend.

Two serious problems marred this picture in the early 1960s: unemployment and underemployment.

DECLINE IN NONFARM WORK WEEK

By 1975, the average work week is expected to be 37 hours.

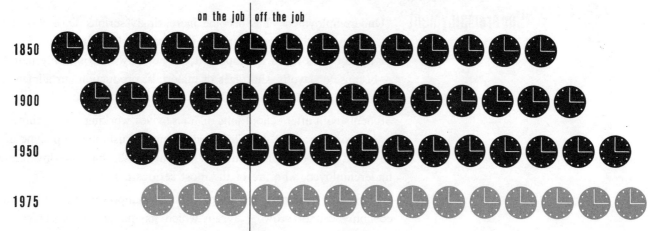

Each symbol represents 12 hours.

Unemployment averaged between 5 and 6 per cent of the civilian labor force—or between 3.5 and 4 million workers. In the recession year of 1961, it reached 4.8 million, or 6.7 per cent of the civilian labor force. It hit Negroes and young people the hardest. The rate of unemployment for Negroes was more than double the rate for whites. Among 16- and 17-year-olds—including large numbers of school dropouts—unemployment reached a record 18 per cent in 1961 and declined only slightly, to 16 per cent, in 1962.

UNEMPLOYMENT

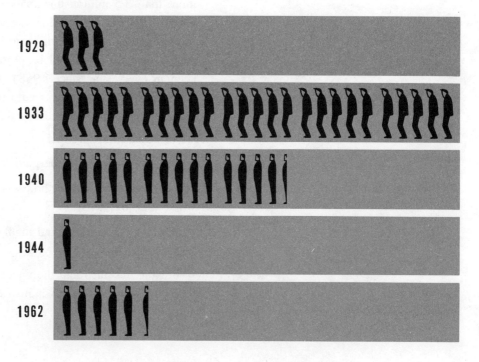

Each symbol represents 1 per cent of the civilian labor force.

17

Regionally, joblessness was worst in the coal regions of West Virginia and Pennsylvania, the textile centers of Massachusetts, and the iron-ore area of Minnesota. In vocational terms, it was most severe for unskilled and semiskilled laborers. With about 26 million young people scheduled to enter the labor force in the 1960s, the nation faced a great challenge in training and equipping job-seekers who had neither skills nor education to back them up.

"Underemployment"

"Underemployment" has become increasingly serious since World War II. For every four people out of work in the early 1960s, there were two or three others listed as employed but actually working only part time —because of layoffs, shortages of materials, production curtailments, illness, or simply from personal choice.

Students with after-school jobs or housewives working two or three days a week or during the pre-Christmas shopping rush make up some of the so-called "underemployment." It is not these, but the involuntarily underemployed, who are of the most serious concern.

As long as a large pool of only partly used manpower exists, the nation's economy cannot grow at a rate which its manpower resources make possible.

These problems of unemployment and underemployment are not new. As a matter of fact, only during the peak of the World War II production effort did the unemployment rate ever get below 2 per cent. In 1933, the worst year of the depression, it was 25 per cent. Since 1947, it has bounced up and down, between 3 and 7 per cent.

The labor force of 1975

It is not surprising, then, that most experts in the field agree that unemployment will be a continuing and nagging problem for the sixties and the seventies. Even if by 1975 unemployment should drop to the 4 per cent level on which many of the projections in this study are based, with a projected civilian labor force of 91 million, this would still mean more than 3.5 million unemployed. But with the great surge of young people who will be looking for jobs in the years immediately ahead, and the difficulty of placing them in an economy turning to automation, unemployment might well be more than 4 per cent in 1975 (as it has been in every year since 1958). Only if steps are taken to make the economy more elastic in its adjustment to technological changes and to changes in the labor force can this trend be checked.

As to other future trends:

- People will probably be paid more, as productivity increases.

- They will work shorter hours—37 hours will probably be the average work week by 1975.

- White-collar workers and highly skilled, technically trained personnel will be most in demand.

- But the unskilled and the uneducated will find it increasingly difficult to get jobs in the nation's industries, trades, and services.

18

CHAPTER IV

America's Productive Plant

Two-legged economy

THE AMERICAN INDUSTRIAL ECONOMY stands on two legs. One, described in the preceding chapter, is its labor force. The other, of course, is its productive plant. Consisting of everything from factories and power plants to typewriters and computers, this plant is indispensable to the nation in all its work.

The industrial and commercial facilities which make up this productive plant include coal mines, oil wells, freight cars, harbor installations, tractors, fishing boats, power plants, warehouses, stores, public transportation facilities—and machinery and equipment which are a part of all of these. They include also schools, hospitals, educational institutions, and all civilian governmental facilities, which, since they supply necessary services, are part of the productive resources. Not included are the things people own and use as consumers: their houses, cars, furniture, appliances, and the like.

No one can put an exact price tag on all the machines, equipment, structures, and facilities devoted to nonfarm production. The latest estimate of their worth, made at the end of 1962, placed the value at approximately $725 billion. This was more than double the value (in constant prices) of this productive capacity in 1929. At the present rate of expansion, it is not unlikely that by 1975 the nation will have increased its productive and commercial facilities by more than half.

Farm productive facilities are also an essential part of the total capacity. They are discussed separately in Chapter XIX.

America's high standard of living is made possible by its productive

VALUE OF THE PRODUCTIVE PLANT PER PERSON

In 1950, the nation had $2,875 worth of productive facilities for each citizen. By 1975, this will be close to $5,000 per person.

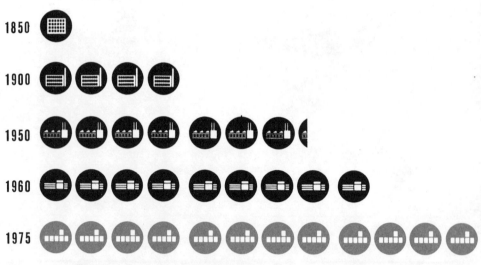

Each symbol represents $400 per person, at 1960 prices.
Includes all civilian, productive, and commercial facilities except farms.

efficiency. Much of the promise of the future lies in the potential of its know-how in manufacturing and distribution—in the efficiency of its productive plant and labor force.

How efficient is it? Estimates of this efficiency are not readily available. One way it has been measured is by what are called "capital-output" ratios—or the amount of production achieved for every $100 invested in machines, factories, and other productive facilities. In 1961, it is estimated that this output was worth $72 (in 1960 prices). In 1929—again using 1960 prices—$100 worth of plant and equipment produced only $47 worth of goods and services. Thus for the same investment in plant and equipment, there was a 53 per cent gain in output between 1929 and 1961.

PRIVATE PRODUCTIVE INVESTMENT AND GNP

In the prosperous year of 1929, private investment in new plant and equipment represented 10.2 per cent of GNP. But in 1962, only 7.4 per cent of GNP was devoted to this purpose.

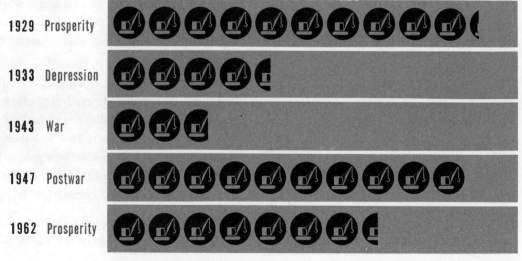

Each symbol represents 1 per cent of GNP.

Despite this optimistic picture, many economists question whether enough of the gross national product is being put into productive facilities to meet the country's expanding needs. In 1929, for example, about 10 per cent of the GNP consisted of private investment in buildings, machines, and other facilities needed for economic growth. In the fifties, this was down to an average of 8.5 per cent. The difference between 10 per cent and 8.5 per cent may not sound very large, but 1.5 per cent of a gross national product of, say, $600 billion means $9 billion less invested in the resources which the nation requires for its growth.

Job ahead

The country is entering a period when it faces great demands for its growing population and rising standards of living. This means more food, clothing, cars, houses, and other necessities of modern living. But it also means that billions will have to be spent for schools, hospitals, airports, highways, recreational facilities, water supply, and all the other needs of expanding communities.

If past experience is any guide, there should be little trouble in meeting these needs. World War II achievements are often pointed to as evidence of the country's ability to produce when the need is urgent. In five years —1939 to 1944—annual production of airplanes increased from 5,856 to 96,359. The gross tonnage of merchant ships built in 1944 was 26 times the tonnage built in 1939. A number of new products—synthetic rubber and magnesium, among them—grew phenomenally during the war years. But these impressive records, it must be remembered, were partly due to the use of resources ordinarily devoted to making automobiles, refrigerators, and other peacetime products whose manufacture had been suspended.

Wartime miracle

The manufacturing plant was expanded 50 per cent in the war period, so that the nation could supply both its own and its allies' war arsenal and still maintain decent living standards for its civilian population.

After the war, basic industrial capacity soared. In the three years from 1950 to 1953, steel capacity rose from 100 million tons to 118 million, aluminum capacity from 633,000 tons to 1.1 million, electric utility generating capacity from 63 million kilowatts to 82 million kilowatts.

Advances in technology accounted in large part for the unprecedented industrial feats of the war and postwar years. Undoubtedly, progress in the years ahead will also be the fruit of technical skills.

Research: key to progress

The key to this progress is research. In the early 1960s, spending by industry, government, and private organizations on research totaled more than $14 billion annually, almost triple the expenditure of a decade earlier. This was less than a fourth of the total investment in physical plant and equipment but was equally important in terms of expanding and improving production. Although the federal government supplied most of the funds, about two thirds of the research was actually performed by private industry in the constant competitive race to keep ahead.

Do the results justify such huge expenditures? A run-through of some examples of how this research has paid off in different areas in recent years provides the answer:

• In the home there are automatic washing machines, dishwashers, garbage disposals, no-frost freezers and refrigerators, electric fryers and roasters, paper napkins and cleansing tissues, aerosol containers, plastic squeeze bottles, air conditioning, odor-killing lamps, electroluminescent lighting, power tools and garden equipment, precooked and premixed foods, synthetic fabrics, "fake" furs, plastic substitutes for leather, vinyl wall and floor coverings.

EXPANDING PRODUCTION

Aluminum, frozen foods, plastics and resins and air transport, have been among the fastest growing industries since World War II.

(index: 1946=100)

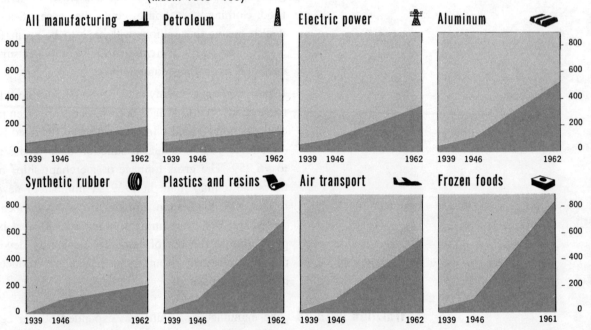

Fruits of research

• Transportation benefits from improved jet airplanes, power brakes and power steering on cars, automatic transmissions, superhighways, compact cars (which originated in Western Europe), air-conditioned buses, "piggyback" truck-and-train combinations, air freight.

• Communication has become easier and more effective with television, transistor radios, nationwide dialing systems, the Telstar communications system, greatly improved publishing techniques, use of color printing in daily papers, transmission of pictures by radio, paperback books, automatic typesetting machines for newspapers, microwave towers to replace cross-country cables, tape recorders, copying machines for reproduction of pictures and text.

• Medicine's advances include control of such childhood diseases as measles and polio; widespread use of antibiotics (penicillin, streptomycin, aureomycin, etc.); development of tranquilizers for relief of emotional tension; new types of anesthetics and painkillers; chemical agents for treatment of tuberculosis, arthritis, and cancer; skin banks, artery banks, blood banks, bone banks; electronic devices for diagnosis and treatment; the mechanical heart; the mechanical kidney.

• Agriculture's productivity has soared as a result of greatly advanced farm equipment, insecticides, fungicides, chemical fertilizers, advanced varieties of seeds and plants, better breeds of cattle and livestock.

• Industry has been made more efficient with fork-lift trucks, conveyor belts, automatic mining machines, diesel engines, better packaging, the spread of automation, electronic controls, computer applications, miniaturization of electronic equipment, ultrasonics, synthetic materials, more efficient use of natural reserves, better plastics, ceramic coatings, faster and more efficient distribution, more imaginative use of credit financing.

Greater output Many, many other examples could be listed. Such advances as these have been largely responsible for the 57 per cent growth in industrial production between 1950 and 1962. They have also resulted in hundreds of thousands of new business enterprises. From 1950 to 1962 there was a net increase of nearly three quarters of a million new business firms. A sidelight to the general expansion is the shifts which have taken place in the location of factories. In 1939 about 33 per cent of the investment in new manufacturing plant and equipment was in the northeastern states. This proportion had dropped to 26 per cent by 1961. Similar drops took place in the north central states—from 38 to 33 per cent. At the same time the proportion of manufacturing located in the South and West increased. In 1939 only 21 per cent of the investment in new manufacturing plant and equipment was in the South. By 1961 this had risen to 28 per cent. Though relatively little manufacturing is located in the western part of the United States, the proportion of spending for new plant and equipment is rising—from 8 per cent in 1939 to 13 per cent in 1961.

NEW MANUFACTURING PLANTS, BY REGION

Gains in new manufacturing capacity have been made in the South and West.

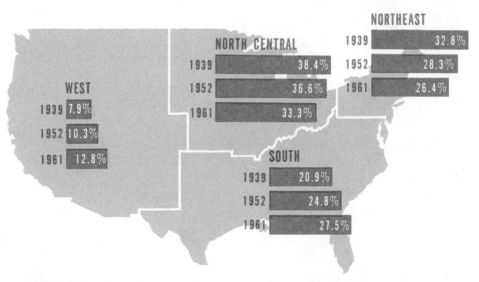

NORTHEAST
1939 32.8%
1952 28.3%
1961 26.4%

NORTH CENTRAL
1939 38.4%
1952 36.6%
1961 33.3%

WEST
1939 7.9%
1952 10.3%
1961 12.8%

SOUTH
1939 20.9%
1952 24.8%
1961 27.5%

Everybody benefits In 1955, J. Frederic Dewhurst wrote in *America's Needs and Resources: A New Survey* of the results of a half century of technological progress: "No period of comparable length in human history has brought such great changes in the variety, quality and quantity of goods and services available for consumption. In many ways those of us now passing middle age have within our lifetime experienced a greater advance in our material standard of living and a more pervasive change in our way of life than occurred in all the previous centuries of Western history."

23

Blueprint for tomorrow American industry has its future already blueprinted for it. Compared to today's investment of $49 billion each year in private plant and equipment, 1975's is expected to exceed $100 billion (in 1960 prices). Whereas today's fastest growing industries have been aluminum, glass containers, natural gas, and air transport, tomorrow's are likely to include nuclear power, electronics, rocketry, cybernetics, and other "space age" technologies.

The biggest problem for the United States will be to make full use of its vast industrial capacity and to maintain an adequate rate of expansion. Only in this way can the promise of better living standards for everyone be fulfilled.

CHAPTER V

Money Earned, Money Spent

FEW ASPECTS OF AMERICA impress the visitor more than the evidences everywhere of its productive power: the immense output of the factories, the variety and quantity of goods in the stores, the endless lines of cars on the streets and highways, and the vast amount of new building and construction. Wherever the visitor looks, he sees highly developed community services, such as schools, highways, hospitals. He also sees personal services provided by repair shops, beauty parlors, barbershops, and many other types of shops and businesses.

The GNP These are representative pieces of a huge national "pie" called the "gross national product," or "GNP"—the total market value of all the goods and services produced by factory workers, businessmen, farmers, professional and other self-employed people, and by local, state, and national governments. The annual GNP is generally accepted as a rough measure of the economic well-being of the country.

It is as if someone sat at an adding machine at the end of each year and totaled the dollar value of all the finished goods and services produced and provided during that year—from the cost of the new school down the street and the family's new car, to the money spent by everybody for groceries at the supermarket and for the services of the policeman on the corner.

How GNP is distributed In 1962, the total GNP was an unprecedented $554.9 billion. Of every $100 of this amount, about $64 represented spending for goods and services for the immediate needs of the country's 187 million citizens.

FLOW OF INCOME AND EXPENDITURES, 1962

in billions

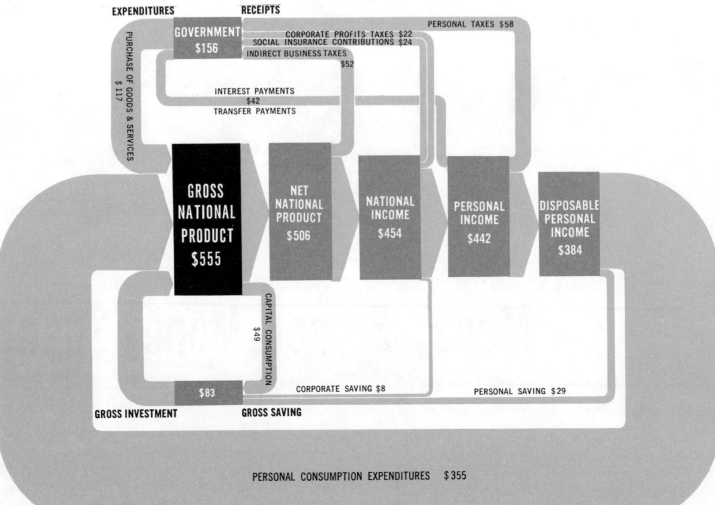

The **gross national product** (the market value of the nation's total annual output of goods and services) amounted to $555 billion in 1962.

When **capital consumption** (the value of machinery and plant used up in production), which amounted to $49 billion in 1962, is deducted,

The **net national product,** $506 billion in 1962, remains.

After deduction of **indirect business taxes** (including miscellaneous adjustments), totaling $52 billion in 1962, which flow to the **government** sector,

National income—$454 billion in 1962—remains.

From national income, **social insurance contributions** ($24 billion) in 1962, and **corporate profits taxes** ($22 billion) go to the **government** sector and **corporate saving** ($8 billion) to **gross** saving.

To the remaining $400 billion in 1962 was added $42 billion in **transfer and interest payments** from **government** to individuals.

Personal income in 1962 thus totaled $442 billion.

From **personal income,** individuals pay **personal taxes** ($58 billion in 1962) to **government**.

This left as **disposable personal income** $384 billion in 1962.

Personal consumption expenditures for goods and services totaled $355 billion in 1962, which left **personal saving** of $29 billion, which went into **gross saving**.

Gross saving amounted to $86 billion, the total of **capital consumption, corporate saving,** and **personal saving.** After adjustment is made for statistical discrepancy and government surplus or deficit, it equals **gross investment** of $83 billion.

The sum of:	billions
Gross investment	$83
Personal consumption expenditures	$355
Government purchases of goods and services	$117
equals **gross national product**	$555 billion in 1962.

Almost $14 consisted of investment in new houses and in new plants, machines, equipment, and inventory needed by industry, business, and agriculture. Slightly over $21 represented government spending for goods and services—including everything from police protection to Jupiter rockets. Net exports of goods and services accounted for slightly less than $1 of the $100.

A look back to 1933

In 1933—low point of the depression—GNP was $56 billion, about one tenth what it was in 1962. This was only slightly more than half the 1929 boom year GNP of $104 billion, a shift that shows how violent was the country's plunge into depression. The 1929 figure wasn't to be surpassed until 1941. Then, with the spending brought on by World War II, GNP soared, reaching $214 billion in 1945. Apart from dips in 1949 and 1954, GNP has risen steadily since 1946.

Inflation's bite

Price changes, of course, have an important effect on the ups and downs of GNP. Only by converting the GNP for all years to "constant dollars," or dollars of the same purchasing power, can a true year-by-year comparison be made. For example, in current prices (or prices of the year shown), GNP rose from $211 billion in 1944 to $329 billion in 1951. But measured in 1960 dollars of equal purchasing power, the rise was only from $373 billion in 1944 to $391 billion in 1951. Obviously, the upward movement of GNP in current prices during this period was attributable largely to rising prices.

Similarly, most of the 891 per cent rise in GNP from 1933 to 1962 was due to inflation. When GNP for both years is expressed in 1960 prices, the growth over this period amounts to only 274 per cent, or a compound rate of about 4.6 per cent per year.

Effect of population changes

The rise in GNP has mirrored the dimensions of a constantly growing national economy. But the country is bigger now than in 1933—61 million more people in 1962—so even though the GNP is higher, it has to be shared by a larger population, a factor that must also be taken into account in considering how significant the growth in total GNP is.

The best measure of real economic growth since 1933 is the rise in GNP per person in constant dollars. This eliminates the effects of both inflation and population increase. In these terms, the gain was 152 per cent for the period 1933-1962, or an annual growth rate of 3.2 per cent.

The figures below dramatize the effects of inflation and population increase on growth of GNP from prosperous 1929 to prosperous 1962:

year	total GNP, billions		per capita GNP	
	current dollars	1960 dollars	current dollars	1960 dollars
1929	$104	$208	$ 854	$1,704
1933	56	145	446	1,150
1944	211	373	1,519	2,697
1951	329	391	2,124	2,533
1962	555	540	2,974	2,894

The GNP growth rate (in constant dollars) has been slower in recent years in the United States than in many other industrialized areas, such as Japan, Italy, France, West Germany, and Western Europe as a whole. This has aroused considerable concern among many Americans.

U.S. AND EUROPEAN GROWTH IN GNP

Much of Western Europe's rapid growth resulted from reconstruction after World War II.

index (1950=100)

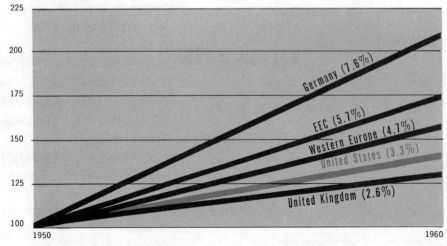

Figures in parentheses are the compounded annual growth rates in GNP for each area, 1950-1960.

Compared with other countries, however, the United States is far in the lead in the value of its output. Its gross national product of $503 billion in 1960 exceeded the $318 billion for all of Western Europe.

Government's changing share

As the country has changed, the make-up, as well as the amount, of GNP has changed. For example, in 1929 three fourths of the nation's output was for personal consumption, compared to only about two thirds now. Also, slightly more of the GNP went into capital investment—to create homes, factories, equipment, school buildings, etc.—in 1929 than in the early 1960s. But the big change has been in the proportion represented by purchases of goods and services by federal, state, and local governments. In 1929, government purchases at all levels accounted for only 11 per cent of total GNP. Today, as mentioned earlier, they account for 21 per cent.

What has happened, obviously, is that government plays a much more important part in the economy now than 30 years ago. During World War II, the share of GNP represented by government spending rose dramatically. At one point, in 1944, as the country built and produced for defense, it was half of total GNP. After the war, the government share dropped—but not to the low prewar levels. Then came the Korean War, and another surge took place in government spending. Since then, government purchases of goods and services as a share of GNP has remained high, leveling off at about 20 per cent.

The expanding role of government in the economy has, of course, increased the need of federal, state, and local governments for money to finance their activities. Much of the need has been filled by increases in personal taxes (income, property, and other taxes paid by individuals), which rose from $4.7 billion in 1929 to $56.6 billion in 1962 (in 1960 dollars). This was equivalent to a rise from $39 per person in 1929 to $303 per person in 1962.

With the nation's output constantly on the upgrade, one would conclude that the average person and the average family have benefited. And they have.

28

PERSONAL INCOME TAKEN BY TAXES

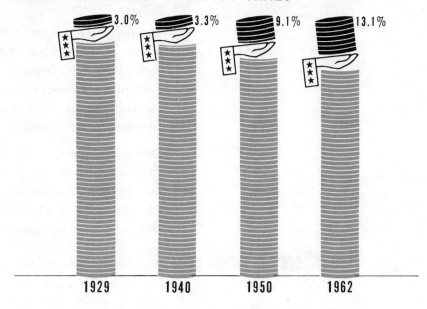

3.0% 3.3% 9.1% 13.1%

1929   1940   1950   1962

More money to spend In terms of personal disposable income per capita (in 1960 dollars), today's consumer is more than twice as well off as the consumer in the worst years of the depression of the 1930s. He is about 18 per cent better off than the consumer in the peak year of World War II. If 1962's total personal income of $433 billion (in 1960 dollars) were divided equally among all Americans, the average person's share would be $2,319, a gain of $1,000 over 1940's average personal income. After paying his taxes, the average person in 1962 had $2,016 left to spend or save—$740 more than in 1940.

AVERAGE INCOME PER PERSON (after taxes)
(in 1960 dollars)

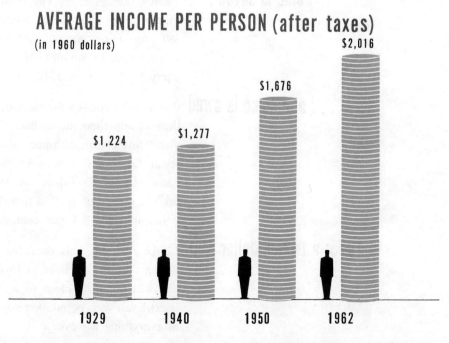

$1,224 $1,277 $1,676 $2,016

1929   1940   1950   1962

As individual incomes have increased, family incomes (in 1960 dollars) also have been pushing upward. In 1947, for example, half the families in the country had incomes of slightly over $4,000 a year. Half had less than that. By 1962, the median family income was $5,850. Net gain for the 14-year period was 46 per cent. Average family income, which differs from median income because of the effect of large in-

29

comes at the high end of the scale, came to $7,011 in 1962 (in 1960 dollars).

The degree of prosperity individuals enjoyed in the early 1960s depended partly on where they lived. Those in the cities had higher incomes than those living in rural areas. People in New England and California had higher incomes than those in the South. There were also racial differences. Median income of Negro families in 1962 was 47 per cent lower than that of whites.

Despite the general prosperity, poverty had by no means disappeared from the national scene in 1962. An estimated 9.4 million families, or one fifth of all families, had incomes of $3,000 or less. In 1947, however, one third of all families had incomes below the $3,000 level in terms of today's purchasing power.

Where the money goes

With their income going up, people have tended to change their spending habits. They now spend far more for services—medical care, dry cleaning, travel, recreation, education, and various items of personal business—than at any time in the past. Just after World War II, they spent 31 cents out of every dollar for these purposes; in the early 1960s, this figure was up to 41 cents.

Spending on nondurable items (food, clothing, household supplies) is about triple that for hard goods (household appliances, cars, furniture). Even so, spending for nondurable items today represents only 45 cents out of every dollar spent, compared to 58 cents in 1946. As incomes go up, people tend to spend larger percentages of their incomes for expensive durables and smaller percentages for food and clothing.

Some is saved . . .

Family savings today (in 1960 prices) are more than double the savings of families in 1929. Roughly $7 out of every $100 people have left after taxes go into savings accounts, insurance, investments, and other forms of savings. In 1929, savings took about $2 less out of every $100 than in 1962.

. . . and some is owed

Going into debt is a far more common—and acceptable—practice today than at any time in the nation's history. Total consumer indebtedness (including charge accounts, single-payment loans, service charges, personal loans and other installment debt) was $63 billion in 1962, compared to $7 billion in 1950. Current indebtedness amounts to 16.5 per cent of total disposable income (income after taxes), compared to only 3.4 per cent in 1950.

In 1975: a trillion dollar GNP

Looking ahead, it is probable that at the present rate of growth, the nation's GNP, expressed in 1960 prices, will reach $780 billion in 1970, and will be fairly close to a trillion dollars ($955 billion) five years later! Even with population approaching 235 million, there will be more of everything for everyone.

The nation's investment in factories, machinery, office buildings, stores, roads, airlines, and other industrial and commercial facilities will increase substantially. And the government's part in the economy will be strong. From 1929 to 1962, for example, total federal, state, and local spending for goods and services rose from $8.5 billion to $118 billion a year. This trend will continue.

30

HOW CONSUMERS SPEND THEIR MONEY

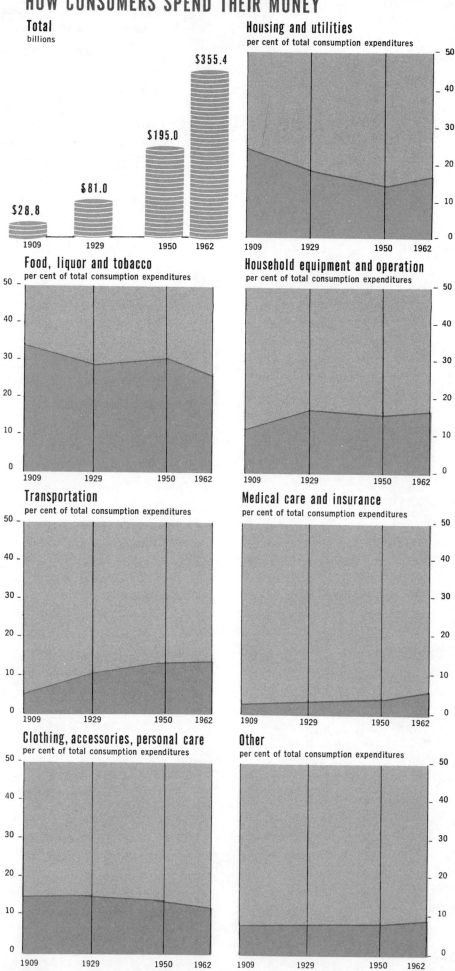

Total
billions

$28.8   1909
$81.0   1929
$195.0   1950
$355.4   1962

Housing and utilities
per cent of total consumption expenditures

Food, liquor and tobacco
per cent of total consumption expenditures

Household equipment and operation
per cent of total consumption expenditures

Transportation
per cent of total consumption expenditures

Medical care and insurance
per cent of total consumption expenditures

Clothing, accessories, personal care
per cent of total consumption expenditures

Other
per cent of total consumption expenditures

31

If past experience is a guide, consumers will spend more of their incomes on travel and recreation, education, medical care, and insurance.

House construction will boom. Purchase of appliances, cars, and furniture will continue to go up. But the share of family income spent for food and clothing is not likely to rise.

Resources for tomorrow

There will be shortages—of housing, medical care, roads, and other vital needs. Despite its phenomenal growth, the country will be constantly confronted with the task of pacing its economic expansion to the requirements of a growing nation. The evidence is clear that it has the resources to do so.

CHAPTER VI

Eating, Drinking, Smoking

WITH GOOD REASON, Americans like to think of themselves as the best-fed people in the world. And, by most nutritional standards, they are. Thanks to lush land resources, advanced agricultural methods, and high consumer incomes, practically the only limits on what the average American eats are imposed by his own personal tastes and preferences. As a visit to any supermarket will demonstrate, the nation's market basket overflows with the bounty of its soil.

Given these rich resources, American families are free to alter their food-buying habits and consumption as they choose. And alter them they do. In recent years, there have been changes in the amounts of food they consume, the types of food they eat, the forms in which food products are purchased, and the ways in which they are stored in the home. All this has been happening while the proportion of family expenditures that goes for food has been declining.

Why Americans now eat less

Americans are eating less now than at any time since annual food consumption statistics were first collected in 1909. In 1961, the average per person was slightly less than 4 pounds of food daily, or 1,455 pounds (retail weight) in the entire year. In 1909, annual consumption per person was 1,616 pounds, a figure which since then has been equaled only in the years 1944-1946. Otherwise, the trend in food consumption, in both pounds and calories, has been gradually and almost consistently downward.

There are two explanations for this. One is the obesity-consciousness of American men and women. Warned by doctors that excess weight

33

can be the route to disease and shortened life expectancy, Americans have been counting their calories with conscientious zeal.

The other reason is the age "mix" of the nation's population. Since children usually eat less than adults, per capita food consumpion falls as the proportion of children in the nation increases. For example, in 1950, when 27 per cent of the population was under 15, the average consumption per person was 1,502 pounds of food for the year. But in 1960, when the number of persons under 15 had risen to 31 per cent of the population, average annual food consumption was down to 1,467 pounds—35 pounds less than 10 years earlier.

The food bill U.S. shoppers allocate a bigger proportion of their spending for food than for any other single purpose. About 21 cents out of every dollar goes for food and nonalcoholic beverages. Add the spending for liquor and the figure goes to 24 cents. Add what goes for cigarettes and other tobacco products, and the total is 26 cents.

No matter how families feel about the size of their food bills, the fact is that families are better off now than ever before—thanks to rising incomes. Until recent years, the total spent for food, liquor, and tobacco had averaged nearly one third of all consumer spending, compared to today's 26 per cent.

SPENDING FOR FOOD, LIQUOR, AND TOBACCO

Food, liquor, and tobacco take a smaller portion of consumer expenditures than ever before.

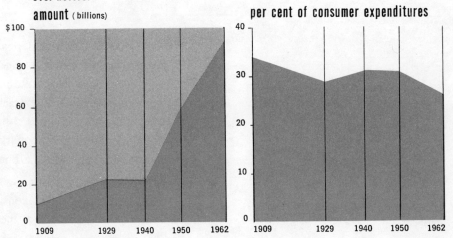

Out to dinner Eating out is a favorite American pastime—one which adds considerably to consumer food expenditures. City families spend $1 or more for restaurant meals, snacks, lunches, and the like for every $3.50 spent on food consumed at home. As families get bigger, this treat is not quite so common—probably because children add to the bill. Nevertheless, Americans do like to eat out and there is no evidence that they are cutting down on spending for this pleasure. In 1962, they spent more than $18 billion for restaurant meals and $64 billion for food consumed at home.

The road to good nutrition Even though people are eating smaller quantities and even though a smaller percentage of their spending goes for food, their diets are generally nutritious, their meals balanced, and their choice of foods in accordance with good standards of health.

What has happened is that in the last quarter century or so, Americans have learned to temper their appetites with a wise choice of health-giving foods. Nowadays, one finds fewer potatoes, cereals, and other starches on the dinner table, and more meat, poultry, fish, fruits, and vegetables.

CHANGING FOOD PREFERENCES

People's diets are more healthful in recent years than in the years before World War I, because they eat more protein foods, such as dairy products, meat, and poultry.

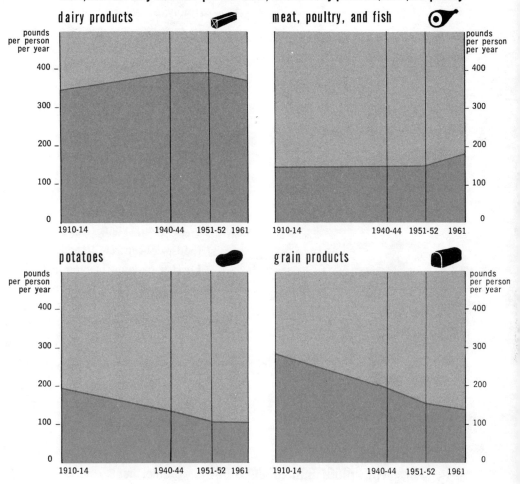

Between 1950 and 1960, the per person consumption of meat, poultry, and fish increased by 23 pounds per year; the consumption of citrus fruits and tomatoes by 7 pounds. But the average person ate 21 pounds less of grain products; 14 pounds less of dairy products; 3 pounds less of dried beans and peas, nuts, and soya products; 6 pounds less of potatoes.

This is a long-term trend, going back at least a generation, when awareness of nutritional needs began to change the nation's eating habits. Spreading education contributed to this awareness. Rising incomes enabled millions of families to put knowledge of good nutrition into practice.

Shifts in eating habits have made diets richer in such important nutrients as proteins, calcium, iron, thiamine, riboflavin, and niacin. On the other hand—partly because of a slight falling off in consumption of vegetables, dairy products, and eggs—diets have less vitamin A and ascorbic acid in them now than they had a generation ago. It is hoped that by 1970 this deficiency will be remedied.

Man has improved on nature in supplying nutritional needs. For over 30 years, synthetic vitamins have enriched bread, flour, other cereals, milk, margarines, salt, and some canned foods. In some instances, these additives replace nutrients removed in food processing. In others, they add to natural ingredients of the product. Strict government controls regulate the use of these chemical additives, including preservatives, flavors, and coloring.

Despite their changing diets, Americans still get a more than ample supply of calories—the energy units supplied by food. In 1962, the average per person was 3,170 calories a day, an amount exceeded only in Australia, Canada, Denmark, Iceland, Ireland, New Zealand, and the United Kingdom. Obviously, millions of Americans absorb many more calories each day than they actually need. The campaign against obesity is making headway, but it is by no means over.

"Built-in maid service" As the decade of the sixties began, "built-in maid service" was a positive advantage to the housewife in shopping for food. Consumption of frozen foods had almost tripled in the preceding decade—from 22 pounds per person in 1950 to 61 pounds 10 years later. In 1960, consumption of such items as TV dinners and frozen pies was 15 times as great as in 1950. Cake mixes, biscuit and pastry mixes, dehydrated foods, concentrated foods, and other products lessened cooking chores. Food packaging became a combined art and science, designed to meet every need, from convenient storage to simple serving. The use of atomic energy to preserve foods without canning, freezing, or refrigeration came closer to general use, as the Army demonstrated that with bacon, for example, the process was efficient and safe.

A revolution in food preparation was under way. Processors had learned how to enrich food. Consumers had learned how to choose and eat balanced diets. Now came an era when the task of preparing food—which once took half the time of the housewife—required far less of her work day.

The liquor and tobacco bill Two other items usually included in the food budget—though not actually foods—are liquor and tobacco. The nation's annual liquor bill now exceeds $10 billion, its tobacco bill is over $7.5 billion. On a per capita basis, the liquor bill now runs about $56 a year, down from the peak of $60 per year 15 years ago. Spending for tobacco reached an all-time high of $42 a year per person in 1962. (In 1933, it was only $10.)

Based on the total population, hard liquor consumption in 1961 averaged 1.2 gallons a person, an increase of two tenths of a gallon over 1950. Beer consumption per person dropped by 2 gallons to 15 gallons a year in the same interval, while wine consumption, at nine tenths of a gallon per person, remained unchanged. Surprisingly, the drinking of alcoholic beverages, except wine, has never reached the average levels of pre-prohibition days.

Cigarette habit Tobacco is another story. In 1925, cigarette smoking averaged 50 packs annually per person 15 years of age and over. By 1950, the annual average was 166 packs per person; by 1958, 185 packs per person; by 1961, 199 packs per person. In the same 36-year period, cigar smoking dropped from an average of 87 cigars per person per year to 56 cigars. Consumption of smoking and chewing tobacco and snuff went from about 4 pounds per person to less than a pound during the same period.

ANNUAL TOBACCO CONSUMPTION PER ADULT

Americans 15 years old and over smoked an average of four times as many cigarettes per person in 1961 as in 1925. Consumption of other forms of tobacco declined.

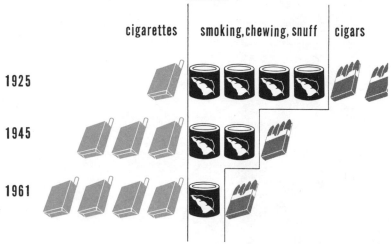

| | cigarettes | smoking, chewing, snuff | cigars |

Each pack of cigarettes represents 50 packs of 20 cigarettes each.
Each can of tobacco represents 1 pound of tobacco.
Each pack of cigars represents 50 cigars.
Note: A person 15 years old and over is considered an adult.

The use of cigarettes had soared to such a point by the mid-1950s that 6 out of every 10 men and 3 out of every 10 women between 25 and 44 years of age were regular smokers. It was estimated that the proportion of smokers among women between 18 and 24 years old was the same as among women in the older age group, and the proportion among men 18 to 24 was only slightly less than that among older men. There was strong evidence, too, that the cigarette habit among high school and junior high school youths was widespread.

While there were differences of opinion, many medical authorities warned that heavy smoking was one cause of lung cancer and a contributing factor in circulatory diseases and other disabilities. A commission appointed by the President to study the problem reported early in 1964 that there was a definite relationship between smoking and susceptibility to cancer and to heart, lung, and other diseases.

The commission, which was made up of scientists and doctors, also said that the younger one is when he begins to smoke, the greater are his chances of falling victim to one of these diseases. While there has thus far been no other U.S. government action to discourage the use of cigarettes, the British and Italian governments have taken positive measures to reduce cigarette smoking, particularly among young people.

Food's future Coming back to food, Americans can feel confident that the nation moves into the sixties amply supplied with food resources, both for themselves and for sharing with nations abroad. No one doubts that there is enough to wipe out nutritional deficiencies which persist, particularly among the lowest income groups. More education is needed to stimulate consumption of fruits, vegetables, and dairy products. In general, however, as the nation's living standards rise and as the gospel of good nutrition spreads, it seems clear that as well-fed as they are today, Americans can look forward confidently to even better diets in the years ahead.

CHAPTER VII

Housing for 55 Million Families

U.S. BUILDERS toppled a 24-year-old record in 1949. More than 1 million new nonfarm houses and apartments were started that year, eclipsing the previous record of 937,000 nonfarm housing "starts" in 1925, and launching the nation on an era of unprecedented home construction. Of all the accomplishments of the post–World War II era, none is of greater importance and of more lasting significance to the nation's families.

Year after year since 1949, over 1 million nonfarm dwelling units have been built. In 1959, a new record was reached, with the construction of more than 1.5 million nonfarm dwellings. Since then, the number has ranged from 1.25 to 1.5 million per year. The results of this phenomenal performance can be seen in the spreading sprawl of "suburbia" on the fringes of every major city.

Most of the new dwelling units built since World War II have been single-family houses. But in the early 1960s a boom in apartment housing developed. In 1962, 1 out of every 3 dwelling units built was an apartment, compared to 1 out of 10 in 1955.

Total dwellings in 1960: 58 million The nation had 46 million dwellings at the beginning of the fifties. Ten years later, in 1960, the total came to 58.3 million. Thus, in a single decade, the housing supply had increased by 27 per cent. This was accomplished despite the fact that 4.5 million housing units were torn down or abandoned, either because they were unfit to live in or because room had to be made for more modern buildings, for roads, or for other purposes.

INCREASES IN NONFARM HOUSING AND POPULATION

About 12 million nonfarm houses and apartments were built in 1950-1959 to handle a population growth of 36 million. Two million additional units were shifted to the nonfarm dwelling unit inventory because of a change in definition of farm residence.

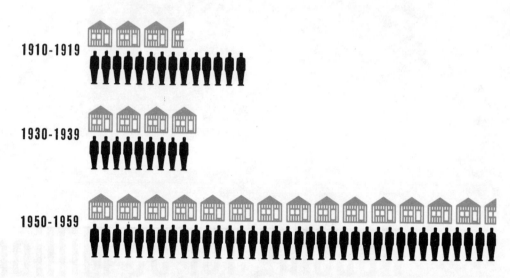

1910-1919

1930-1939

1950-1959

Each house symbol represents 1 million nonfarm houses and apartments added to the existing supply. Each man symbol represents an increase of 1 million people living in nonfarm areas.

Cost reaches $25 billion a year

Prodigious sums were spent to achieve this growth—more than $25 billion in 1962 alone. In recent years, construction of new dwellings has accounted for about 4.5 per cent of GNP.

Houses and apartments and the land they stand on represent about 27 per cent of the national wealth. Nearly 30 per cent of invested capital goes for materials and labor to build houses and apartments. These billions of dollars invested in housing constitute an important yardstick in measuring the level and trend of American living standards.

Second biggest item of family spending

Next to food, housing is the most important item of family spending. In 1962, an average of about 17 per cent of family expenditures went for housing—rent or mortgage payments, basic structural repairs, and utilities—compared to about 13 per cent in 1946.

What a family gets for its housing dollars varies widely, of course. City homes are generally better equipped and in better condition than farm homes. New houses have better equipment than older ones, but they may lack the spaciousness of the old houses. Houses in the North and West are generally of higher quality than elsewhere.

Unlike many houses in Western Europe, most American housing does not suffer the handicap of having been used too long by too many generations of occupants. In some parts of Western Europe, the average age of dwellings is at least 50 years; in some, over 100 years. In the United States, the average age of existing dwellings is under 30 years. Moreover, the prolonged construction boom increased the proportion of homes less than 10 years old from 21 per cent in 1950 to 28 per cent in 1960.

Ramblers, Cape Cods

Climate, tradition, taste, available materials all affect housing design. In recent years, the rambler and the split level have enjoyed tremendous popularity. There has been a strong revival of the traditional Cape Cod and colonial designs. Houses built in attached or semidetached style are popular in cities. Garden-type apartment developments, often with swimming pools, are popular in the suburbs. A unique development in U. S. housing has been adoption of mobile homes and trailers as a way of life by retired families, people in construction or other work that takes them from place to place, and young couples. In 1962, 175,000 new housing units, or over 12 per cent of all new units, were in this category.

What houses cost What kind of homes were American families buying in 1962? Generally, they chose five- or six-room houses. The cost of building their homes averaged $14,325, excluding cost of land and settlement charges. Despite the trend to compactness, millions of U. S. families lived in big houses or apartments—eight or more rooms. In 1960, about 4 million dwellings, or 7 per cent of all occupied dwellings, were of this size.

HOUSING PICTURE, 1960

From four to seven million houses in 1960 still lacked one or more of these conveniences: running water, private flush toilets, and private baths.

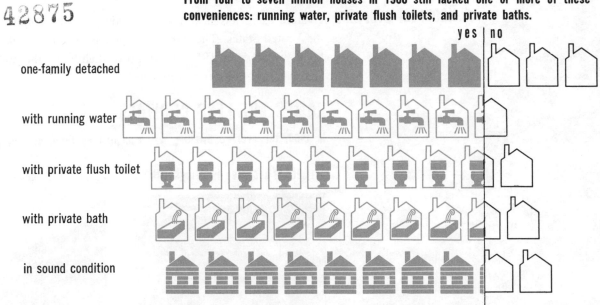

yes | no

one-family detached

with running water

with private flush toilet

with private bath

in sound condition

Each symbol represents 10 per cent of all dwelling units.

In spite of the boom in home building, the condition of large numbers of U. S. homes in the early 1960s left much to be desired. Here are some of the shortcomings which existed in 1960:

- 7 per cent lacked running water.

- 13 per cent had no private flush toilet.

- About 15 per cent were without private bath.

- Central heat was lacking in about a third of the dwellings. (This is not, of course, a shortcoming in houses in the far South.)

- About a fifth of all homes had no telephone.

Generally, these shortcomings were more widespread in farm homes than in city homes.

Improvement has been made in over-all housing conditions in recent years. The Census Bureau estimated in 1950 that about 10 per cent of the nation's houses were "dilapidated"—meaning that they no longer provided safe and adequate shelter and, thus, needed replacement or extensive renovation. More than one fourth of all dwellings lacked one or more of these items of equipment: inside private toilet, bath, running water, electricity, heating equipment. By 1960, however, only 5 per cent of the dwelling units were classified as "dilapidated" and only 15 per cent lacked adequate plumbing, electricity, or heating equipment.

Progress in construction Other changes have occurred. New building materials have appeared: better insulation, pressed wallboards, radiant heat panels, packaged kitchens and bathrooms, prefabricated door and window frames, standardized building components, asbestos and vinyl flooring material, and a great variety of other products. Assembly-line methods have been brought to building sites. Some—not all—of the archaic building methods and techniques of former years have been abandoned. Dishwashers, freezers, air conditioners, and other equipment previously limited to only the most expensive homes are now included as standard items in moderately priced new homes and are tending to become standard items in new apartments.

Room for everyone Overcrowding has never been a widespread or continuing problem in the United States. The number of persons occupying the average U. S. home was 3.5 in 1950. It dropped slightly in the following decade, and averaged 3.4 persons in 1960.

HOMES ARE LESS CROWDED

In 1960, the average dwelling was occupied by three or four persons.

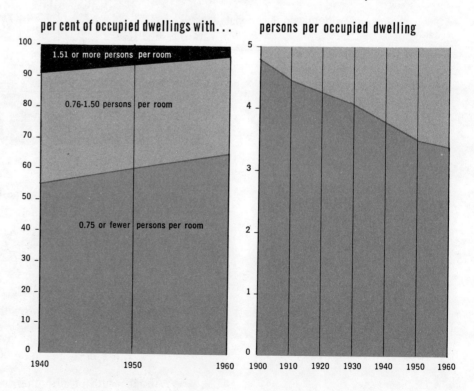

per cent of occupied dwellings with...

persons per occupied dwelling

Paying for a house Home financing is an area in which the United States has pioneered. For many years, Americans have been able to borrow money easily and at favorable rates to buy a home—in some instances, with only a token down payment.

42

Interest rates on first mortgages for one-family homes have been slowly declining over the past 20 years or so, at a time when the general price level has been rising. The median interest rate for this type of mortgage was 6 per cent in 1940; 20 years later, it had dropped to 5.1 per cent. In 1960, fewer than 5 out of 100 owners of one-family houses paid over 6 per cent mortgage interest. But 20 years earlier, 8 out of 100 were paying more than 6 per cent. Things were quite different in the 1890s; at the beginning of that decade, 1 out of 4 homeowners paid 8 per cent or more on their first mortgages.

The mortgage debt of $169 billion on nonfarm, noncommercial housing in 1962 was more than seven times that of 1946. This rising mortgage debt is reflected in the increase in home ownership and the decrease in the number of homes completely paid for. In 1950, 56 of every 100 homes were mortgage-free; by 1960, only 43 out of every 100 were not mortgaged. On the other hand, in 1960, 62 of every 100 homes were "owner"-occupied (with or without mortgage), in contrast to 55 per cent in 1950.

The patterns of the future can be confidently predicted, both in terms of what the nation will need in housing and what types of dwellings will be built.

Needed: 2 million new homes a year

As to the needs, the probabilities are that by 1975 a minimum of about 2 million new dwelling units will be built annually to keep up with the coming population expansion and to replace units which have been torn down. By 1970, the nation will have about 68 million dwellings, compared to 1960's 58 million; by 1975, there will probably be 75 million, to serve the nation's 68 million households. The prediction that there will be more houses than households is based on the assumption that the present vacancy rate of about 10 per cent will continue and that there will be an increase in the number of families owning summer houses or cottages.

Millions of dwellings now in use will be torn down, mostly because they are beyond economical repair or rehabilitation. If present trends continue, only about 1 out of 50 houses will be considered "dilapidated" by 1975.

HOME OWNERSHIP INCREASING

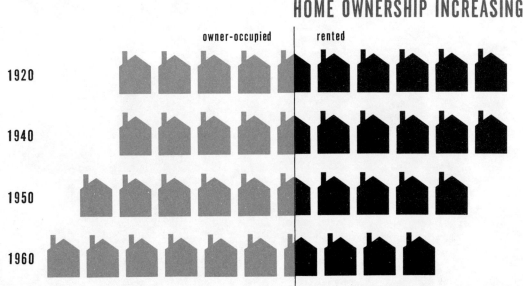

owner-occupied | rented

1920

1940

1950

1960

Each symbol represents 10 per cent of all occupied units.

New materials—plastics, metals, synthetics, new types of glass—will come into more widespread use as the building industry tries to keep up with the needs. Mass production methods, still in their infancy in housing, will be refined and improved, and factory fabrication of both components and entire units will probably be employed much more intensively than today.

Housing will get bigger and more important

Now a $25 billion industry, housing by 1975 will be a $45 billion business. It will continue to have a strong effect on the economy, and its contributions to rising standards of living for almost everyone will make it of prime importance to the nation.

CHAPTER VIII

Making a House a Home

WHAT HAPPENS when a family sets up housekeeping? First, of course, there has to be furniture: beds, tables, chairs, and the rest. Then there must be appliances: everything from the kitchen toaster to the automatic drier in the basement. A family soon begins to worry about financial and legal problems, so money must be set aside for such items as homeowner's insurance—fire, storm damage, and other types of coverage—interest on mortgages and loans, and legal counsel, in case it is needed. In due time, cleaning, repair, and maintenance expenses make their demands on income. Maybe there is a maid, a cleaning woman, or a part-time gardener to be paid. And a telephone is practically indispensable for most households.

Running a house is expensive

Altogether, these items take about one dollar out of six in the average family's spending. Or, to put it in even more basic terms, most U. S. families spend about 16 or 17 cents out of every dollar for furniture and equipment and for running and maintaining the house. The percentage has not varied much in recent years. As a matter of fact, the share of the household dollar spent on household equipment and operation was almost identical in 1962 and in 1929.

What families get for this spending is a lot different today from a generation ago, however. Here is evidence of how times have changed:

• Modern houses are more functional, easier to keep clean, and simpler to run. But they don't have as much space as homes of 40 or 50 years ago.

• Appliances have been created for almost every conceivable use: wash-

SPENDING FOR HOUSEHOLD OPERATIONS

In 1962, Americans spent a record amount of $59 billion (an average of $1,100 per dwelling unit) to equip, furnish, and operate their homes.

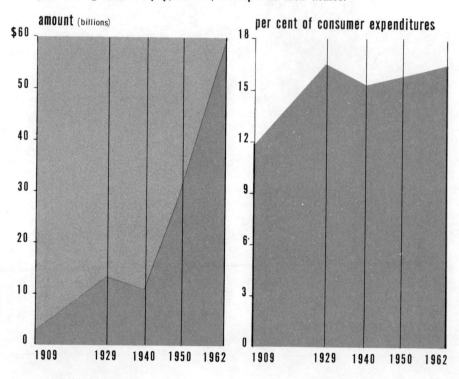

ing, drying, freezing, cooling, mixing, ironing, shoe shining, hair drying, broiling, baking, toasting, cleaning, polishing, heating, air conditioning, humidifying, dehumidifying, painting—just about every household chore except making the bed!

● Furniture is simpler, easier to clean, built for basic comfort—though not, as in the "old" days, necessarily designed to last a lifetime.

● New kinds of floor coverings, such as vinyl tile, have replaced in part the traditional rugs of wool and cotton.

● Houses are sold with "built-ins"—bookcases, kitchen shelves and cabinets, appliances, storage areas, even desks and chests.

● People lean toward "do-it-yourself" repairs and redecorating. They are prone to do their own painting, electrical and plumbing repairs, furniture refinishing, home maintenance and construction, and many other tasks which in the past demanded the services of paid craftsmen.

● There is a greatly expanded use of credit. Furniture, appliances, and houses themselves are bought with only small down payments, with the purchasers not reluctant to spread the balance over a period of many months or years.

How the money is spent As a result of these and other changes, there have been basic shifts in how the household operations dollar is spent.

Of all the changes, none has been as significant as the spending on household "business." In most households, insurance is taken out, or money borrowed, or contracts signed, or agreements made for one purpose or another. For householders, this is the "business" side of equipping and maintaining their homes and, in many respects, it is like running a business.

46

Total annual expenditures for household business purposes (including burial expenses) almost tripled between 1950 and 1962—from $8.4 billion to $22.7 billion. By 1962, they were nearly 40 per cent of total spending for household equipment and operation, compared with 27 per cent in 1950. More than any other single factor, interest on consumer debts accounted for the jump. (Total consumer debts rose from $21 billion to $63 billion in these 12 years.)

UPS AND DOWNS IN HOUSEHOLD SPENDING

The fastest growing item of household expense in recent years has been for financial, legal, insurance, and similar purposes.

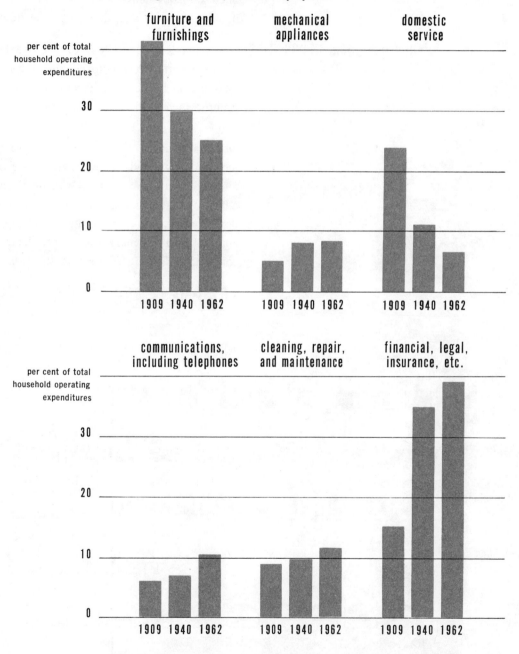

Another big increase has been in the amount spent for "communications"—telephone, telegrams and cablegrams, writing supplies, and postal services. In dollars, this spending in 1962 was two and one half times the 1950 figure, having risen from $2.5 billion to $6.2 billion.

The total spent for cleaning, repair, and maintenance doubled—from $3.25 billion in 1950 to $6.5 billion in 1962.

Spending for appliances (refrigerators, washers and driers, freezers, ironers, air conditioners, etc.) rose moderately in the 1950s. About 8 per cent of total household operating expenditures went for these conveniences in 1962, compared to 13 per cent 12 years earlier. The drop was evidence that, temporarily at least, families had caught up with their needs for these items and also were able to buy them at lower prices.

Furniture and furnishings also accounted for a smaller share of household operating expenditures in 1962 than in 1950. By 1962, they consumed only 25 cents of each dollar spent to run the average home, compared with 33 cents of each household operations dollar in 1950.

Such statistics help to measure the nation's economic progress in the place where it means the most—the home.

Luxuries become necessities

For example, at least four out of five homes now boast refrigerators, gas or electric kitchen stoves, and telephones. Three out of four homes have washing machines. Except in the homes of the very lowest income groups, such work savers and conveniences are standard home equipment.

Other appliances are beginning to lose their luxury labels. More and more homes include dishwashers, waste disposers, **driers**, freezers, and air conditioners as part of their regular equipment. In millions of kitchens a large variety of smaller appliances is found. Most of these are of recent development, but are nevertheless getting wide acceptance. They include automatic can openers, rotisseries, electric bakers and fryers, automatic coffeemakers, knife sharpeners, electric knives, and mixers.

EQUIPMENT AND APPLIANCES IN HOMES, 1960

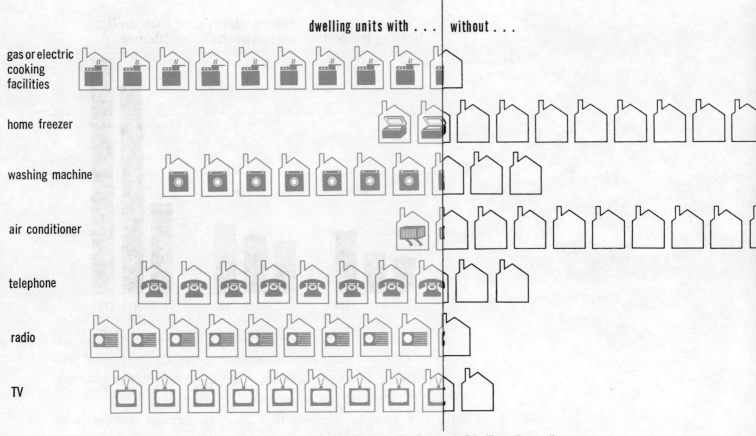

dwelling units with . . . | without . . .

gas or electric cooking facilities

home freezer

washing machine

air conditioner

telephone

radio

TV

Each symbol represents 10 per cent of dwelling units reporting.

Furniture and furnishings

Home furnishings have also gone through a significant transition. Sales of modern lawn and patio furniture have increased more than sales of any other type of furniture, partly because of the imaginative and practical developments in using wood, aluminum, steel, plastics, and reed and rattan, but mainly because of the heavy movement out of the city to the suburbs and the consequent need for this type of furniture. New trends and designs in interior furniture have brought a minor revolution in concepts of comfort and décor. The old kitchen pantry has given way to attractive wood and metal cabinets, designed to blend with built-in sinks, dishwashers, ovens, and surface burners.

Developments such as these have resulted from rising incomes and ability of families to purchase equipment and furnishings previously limited to upper income groups, and also from mass production techniques, which have lowered costs. They also are direct results of the greatly broadened use of consumer credit by millions of families.

SALES OF SOME APPLIANCES INCREASE

Air conditioners, driers, and freezers are currently gaining in favor.

	room air conditioners	clothes driers	home freezers
1950			
1962			

Each symbol represents 300,000 appliances.

Today's home is often praised as one in which household chores can be performed more quickly and efficiently than in the past. To this observation, housewives may be inclined to respond, "Maybe." And they have reasons for their doubts.

SALES OF OTHERS DECREASE

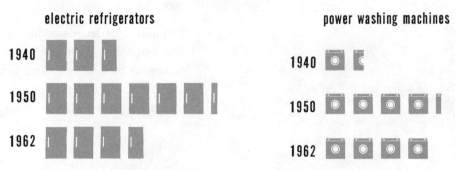

electric refrigerators   power washing machines

| | 1940 | 1950 | 1962 |

Each symbol represents 1 million appliances.

At the turn of the century, domestic servants were readily available to help out with the chores of cooking, cleaning, and homemaking. But by midcentury, millions of former domestics had found more profitable jobs in other types of employment, such as clerking, or working in factories, hotels, or institutions. It is estimated that while in 1900 there was 1 woman domestic for every 13 households, today there are fewer than half that number.

At the same time, housewives must pay more now than in the past for household help, as for everything else. Between 1950 and 1961 alone, wages of domestic workers rose 46 per cent, compared to a 24 per cent rise in living costs in that period.

Housewife's lament

The result of this trend is that most homemakers find that they must perform household tasks by themselves or with the help of husbands and children.

Those tasks have multiplied. Standards of cleanliness are said to be higher now than they used to be. More time is given to care and rearing of children—"togetherness" means work. Millions of wives have gone to work to supplement family incomes, thus limiting the time available for home chores.

So, despite all their appliances and other aids, modern homemakers aren't as free from domestic chores as might be suspected. They still have plenty to do. And they may not have either the time or the help to do the job with ease.

Promise of the future

Tomorrow's house will have more comforts and conveniences. Driers, freezers, air conditioners, dishwashers, and waste disposers will be almost as standard as refrigerators and washers are today. And new products will appear—thermoelectric refrigerators, electroluminescent lights, possibly ultrasonic washing machines. Electronics will play a greater role in homes of the future. For example, scientists predict controls on windows that will close them automatically in the event of a storm.

Household spending for running and equipping the homes of 1975 will inevitably go for the same basic purposes as current spending: furniture, appliances, insurance, interest on loans, legal help, telephones, cleaning, repair and maintenance bills, household help, and communications. Altogether, it is not likely that the share of consumer expenditures devoted to these items will change. That means that about one dollar out of six spent by consumers will continue to go into home operation.

The difference will come in the total amount of money spent on household operation. With incomes rising, people will be able to spend more money on their homes. This is the basic reason why tomorrow's home is going to be better equipped and furnished. It is also why people's material comforts will rise to levels hardly dreamed of a generation ago.

CHAPTER IX

America Dresses Up

JUST AS THEY ARE EATING BETTER, are better housed, and have a greater variety of household furnishings and equipment, Americans are also dressing better than at any time in their history. Most personal wardrobes are well supplied for dress, for work, and for play. Looking at people walking down almost any Main Street, one is struck by the variety, the fashion, and, above all, the informality of their clothing. Today's clothes are a far cry from the bulky dresses, the stiff collars, and the high-buttoned shoes of only a generation or so ago.

Americans adopt informal clothes

Americans spent nearly $42 billion in 1962 on their personal appearance. The types of apparel for which much of this money was expended reflected some very basic shifts in style and fashion tastes.

The accent is no longer on formality, but on relaxed, comfortable clothes. Slacks and sports shirts, sweaters and skirts, moccasins and loafers—these are the major components of the American wardrobe of the sixties. The suit, the necktie, the hat, the "dressy" costume are primarily for office wear or for special occasions.

Changing fashions have also produced a kaleidoscope of color in most wardrobes—men's as well as women's and children's. Particularly in sportswear, men have blossomed out in a variety of gay color combinations that would have astounded their grandfathers.

New fibers and new chemical finishes have produced apparel that is easier to clean, less prone to wrinkling and crumpling, and decidedly more comfortable to wear than clothing of the past.

51

Good news for the family purse

This basic transition in the way Americans dress has been accomplished without straining personal budgets. In fact, for most people, spending for clothing is a smaller proportion of total expenses now than it was a few years ago.

Twenty years ago—in the 1940s—almost $15 out of every $100 spent by consumers went for clothing (including laundry and dry cleaning). Five years after the end of World War II, in 1950, the clothing portion of consumer spending was down to slightly over $11 out of every $100. The reason for the downward trend was that during and immediately after the war people had money to spend, but they encountered shortages of houses, cars, appliances, and other consumer durables. This meant that many people spent more readily for clothes than they would have normally. But when the shortages of durable goods ended, money was channeled away from clothing stores and to the appliance store and the automobile dealer.

WHAT PEOPLE SPEND FOR CLOTHING AND GROOMING

People are spending more on personal appearance than they used to spend. Even so, it takes a decreasing share of total consumer expenditures.

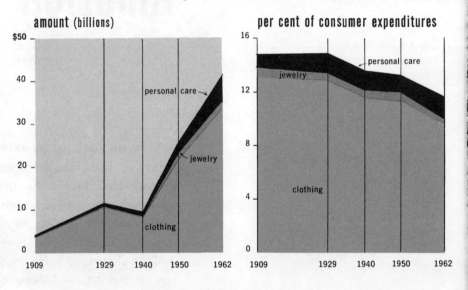

By 1962, clothing expenditures had dropped to an average of $9.33 out of every $100 spent by American families. People still spent generously for apparel. But, because their incomes were higher, they didn't have to allocate as large a share of their spending for this purpose as they had found necessary in the past. It is interesting to compare American experience with that of Western Europe, where expenditures for clothing averaged almost $12 out of every $100 spent by consumers in 1960.

Hair curlers and shaving cream

To the average person, making a good appearance means more than just wearing good clothes; grooming is important, too. How often do women go to the beauty shop or men to the barber? What girl doesn't spend freely for hair curlers and lotions, lipsticks and shampoos, home permanents and nail polish? What young man doesn't buy shaving cream and hair tonics? To these expenditures for personal care must be added the amount spent for jewelry.

Surprisingly, while people have allotted smaller shares of their total spending to clothing and jewelry in recent years, the percentage of their spending devoted to personal care (including, in addition to the items listed above, toothpaste, tissues, hair brushes, mouth washes, toilet soap, and combs) has hit a record high. In 1951, personal care represented $1.25 out of every $100 of consumer spending. In 1962, it amounted to $1.75. The previous high was $1.67 of every $100 spent by consumers in 1944.

Impact of advertising

The explanation? Many new products are available for personal grooming: hair tints, home permanent sets, electric tooth brushes, deodorants, lotions, and countless others. Also, there is no doubt that the massive use of advertising over television and radio and in magazines and newspapers and the dramatic new packaging materials and techniques have greatly stimulated consumer buying. In 1962, at least $300 million (not including radio advertising) was spent to promote these products.

The price of a good appearance

All told, Americans spent about $6.25 billion for personal care in 1962. (If laundry and dry cleaning were included in this category, the total would amount to $9.65 billion.) It was more than twice the amount spent a decade earlier, but part of the increase was, of course, due to higher prices. Slightly more than half the total went for cosmetics and toiletries, the rest for visits to the nation's more than 200,000 beauty parlors and barber shops.

When all spending for clothing, jewelry, and personal care in 1962 is added up, the total is $41.5 billion—61 per cent greater than the $25.8 billion spent in 1950.

The increased emphasis on personal appearance, though largely the result of an over-all rise in the standard of living, also mirrors, in many ways, the changing social structure of the country:

Social trends set fashions

• Migration from farm to city has undoubtedly made people more conscious of personal appearance and more desirous of having "store-bought" clothing.

• The mass media—television, radio, movies, newspapers, magazines—are powerful stimulants to establishing national standards of dress and grooming.

• The growth in the number of white-collar workers—who now outnumber "blue-collar" workers—means more emphasis on good appearance for office work.

• Millions more women, married and unmarried, take jobs outside the home, with obvious effects on their personal wardrobe and beauty needs.

Several personal factors influence families in their spending for clothing, accessories, and personal care. Income is the most important, of course. The higher up the income ladder they go, the more families spend for clothing and personal care.

Other influences include where one lives—whether in a cold or a hot climate; what kind of work the family head does; and the size, composition, and age distribution of the family. (For example, women under 30 spend about twice as much on their wardrobes as women over 50.)

Farm families spend less than city families for clothing. Government surveys in 1959 showed that in 20 large cities annual clothing expenditures ranged from an average of $506 to $598 per family. Average expenditures for clothing ran about $200 less for representative farm families.

Man-made fibers

Of the various influences on the way Americans dress, none has been so striking as the tremendous changes in the textile industry since World War II. Prior to 1945 practically all clothing fabrics were woven from three basic natural fibers: wool, cotton, and silk. The only man-made fibers of any significance were rayon and acetate. As recently as 1950, these represented 90 per cent of all synthetic fibers produced in the United States.

NATURAL VERSUS SYNTHETIC FIBERS

Increasing use of synthetic fibers has not affected consumption of wool, but cotton consumption has dropped somewhat.

average annual civilian consumption per capita

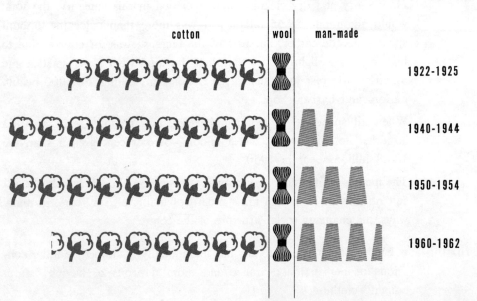

Each symbol represents 3 pounds of textile fibers.

Nylon made a tentative bow just before World War II, but war needs quickly removed it from the civilian market. After the war, nylon forged ahead fast as the first of several thousand synthetic fibers created in chemical laboratories. Only about 50 of these synthetics have had serious consideration for commercial use.

In addition to nylon, among the better known of these are orlon, dynel, and dacron. All have their own special qualities, such as being easy to clean, quick drying, crease resistant, light in weight, fire resistant. Some are used alone, others are blended to make fabrics with particular advantages.

From silk to nylon

As a result of this textile revolution, some of the traditional natural fibers have lost their former prestige. The silk stocking of the thirties has been replaced by the nylon stocking of the sixties, and it is a rare pair of women's hose that is woven from cotton or rayon. More than one fifth of all clothing contains synthetic fibers, twice the proportion of 25 years ago. Consumption of synthetic fibers is about 12.5 pounds per person per year, an increase of 3 pounds since 1950.

NYLON REPLACES SILK IN WOMEN'S HOSIERY

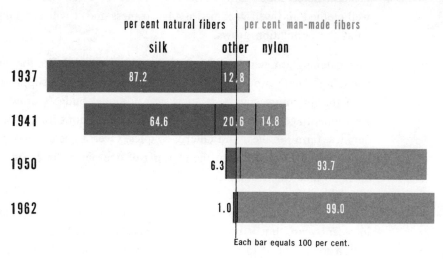

per cent natural fibers | per cent man-made fibers

silk | other | nylon

1937 | 87.2 | 12.8

1941 | 64.6 | 20.6 | 14.8

1950 | 6.3 | 93.7

1962 | 1.0 | 99.0

Each bar equals 100 per cent.

This is not to say that cotton and wool have been eclipsed. Cotton still accounts for three quarters of the fibers used in men's and boys' clothing, four fifths of those used for girls' and infants' wear. Cotton fiber was about 47 per cent of the total of all fibers used in women's and misses' clothing in 1961, down only a little from 50 per cent of the total 5 years earlier. New methods of treating cotton fabrics so that they dry quickly and require little ironing have helped cotton meet the competition of synthetic fibers.

As for wool, the major cutback in its use has been in men's suits, jackets, coats, slacks, and sportswear. Less than 12 per cent of the fibers used in men's clothing in 1961 were wool, compared with 14 per cent in 1956. The increase in the use of synthetics accounts for this downward trend.

A big business Over 5 million people in the manufacturing, trade, and service industries work at the job of filling the needs of their fellow citizens for cloth-

WORKERS IN PERSONAL CARE INDUSTRIES, 1960

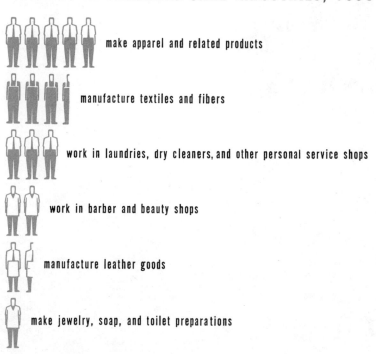

make apparel and related products

manufacture textiles and fibers

work in laundries, dry cleaners, and other personal service shops

work in barber and beauty shops

manufacture leather goods

make jewelry, soap, and toilet preparations

Each symbol represents 250,000 workers (including active proprietors in service shops).
Note: Data for service shops are for 1958.

ing and other goods and services for personal care. Keeping America well clothed and well groomed is big business and it will continue to be so as the population grows.

Just catching up with existing shortcomings could keep the industry humming. There are millions of people whose clothing supply fails to meet the minimum standards suggested in model budgets drawn up by government agencies and private research organizations for city workers' families, farm families, and elderly couples. Over a decade ago, government studies concluded that the clothing of one out of four city families failed to meet the minimum standards.

Needs that must be met This gap between what is owned and what is needed has been narrowed in recent years, but it has not been closed. It cannot be ignored as the nation looks ahead to a future of improving the living standards of all its people.

CHAPTER X

For America's Good Health

MANY OF THE MAJOR ADVANCES in medicine in recent years have had their beginning or flowering in the United States. In the early 1960s, the nation stood on the threshold of even greater medical discoveries, which, if fulfilled, will conquer or control many of today's disabling diseases.

Conquest of major diseases These few examples illustrate the successes of the nation's medical men:

● Use of the Salk and Sabin vaccines for prevention of polio has been so effective that in 5 years—1955 to 1960—the number of polio cases dropped from 29,000 to less than 3,200.

● Tuberculosis, once a major killer, has now been brought under such effective control that the tuberculosis death rate in 1962 was only one fourth that of 12 years earlier.

● Childhood diseases—such as diphtheria, whooping cough, measles, scarlet fever—are no longer the threat they used to be. Some have been practically wiped out.

● Thanks to modern public health measures, one rarely hears of epidemic diseases in the United States any more, except for occasional flare-ups of the still-baffling viruses.

● New drugs for controlling high blood pressure, diabetes, mental diseases, allergies, and other serious afflictions have eased the suffering of millions of people.

As a result, Americans are generally healthier, longer lived, and less susceptible to many serious diseases than ever before in their history.

Cancer, heart disease, mental illness

Medical science has not, however, been uniformly successful in conquering or controlling disease. There are still crippling illnesses which have failed to yield to medical treatment and whose annual toll is mounting.

Two of the worst are heart disease and cancer, the number one and number two killers in the nation. Today's death rate from heart disease is more than two and a half times that of 1900; the death rate from cancer is over twice as high as at the turn of the century. Diseases of the circulatory system affecting the central nervous system rank third in the mortality tables, but new drugs and treatment have brought these under partial control.

While it is not a killer, mental illness is the nation's most prevalent disabling ailment, and one whose incidence is increasing. About half the beds in nonfederal hospitals are occupied by mental patients. In 1960 an estimated 778,000 patients in hospitals and other institutions were suffering from some type of mental illness. More than 223,000 staff physicians, nurses, and other health workers were required to care for those in public hospitals alone.

SOME DEATH RATES UP, OTHERS DOWN

In 1962, 149 people out of 100,000 died from cancer, and 369 out of 100,000 died from heart diseases.

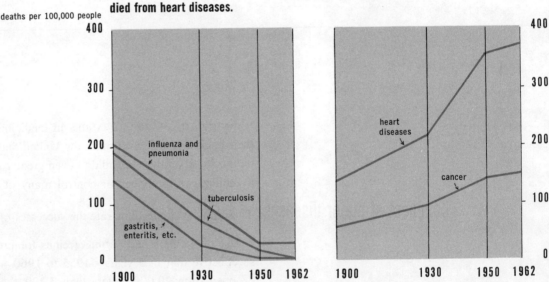

deaths per 100,000 people

Lengthening life expectancy

Weighing the medical successes and failures, there is no question that the former far outbalance the latter. In 1960, average life expectancy of newborn babies had reached an all-time peak: 66.6 years for newborn boys, 73.1 years for their newborn sisters. Putting it another way, baby boys had 20.3 more years of life to look forward to and baby girls 24.8 more years than babies born in 1900.

It is interesting to note that improvement in life expectancy in Western Europe has about paralleled the U.S. advances. Babies born in Western Europe in recent years have about the same life expectancy as American babies. There, too, the Biblical three-score-and-ten is within reach of the boys and has already been exceeded by the girls.

Obviously, conquest of diseases of infancy and childhood has been a major factor in extending life expectancy. The decline in maternal mortality has been an additional factor in lengthening the life expectancy of women.

LIFE EXPECTANCY AT BIRTH

A baby born in 1960 had a life expectancy of 70 years compared with 47 years in 1900 and 60 years in 1930.

Each symbol represents five years.

In 1950, 6.1 white mothers died in childbirth for each 10,000 live births; by 1960, the rate had been cut by more than half. For nonwhite mothers, the rates have remained higher, but the decline has been equally spectacular: 22.2 maternal deaths per 10,000 births in 1950, and 9.8 deaths in 1960.

There has also been a sharp difference in the death rates of white and nonwhite infants. Among white infants, there were 22 deaths per 1,000 live births in 1960; among nonwhites, 43 infant deaths per 1,000 live births. Between 1940 and 1960, the death rate for white infants was cut in half; for nonwhites, the drop was 43 per cent. This continuing gap in the infant death rate is a basic reason why life expectancy of newborn nonwhite babies averages six or seven years less than that of newborn white babies.

What about older people? Has their life expectancy increased over the years? It has—but not very much. In 1960, a 65-year-old man had an average 12.8 years ahead of him, while for women of the same age, life expectancy was 15.8 years. For men, this represented a gain of about a year and a half since 1900; for women, the gain was about three and a half years.

The nation's medical bill

Americans spent about $29 billion for medical care in 1961, including the cost of everything from patients' examinations in doctors' offices to the billions of dollars expended by the federal government on research, hospitals, veterans' care, and other health needs.

This was a huge sum—approaching 6 per cent of the nation's gross national product. It was almost two and a half times the dollars spent in 1950.

If each $100 of medical care expenditures in 1961 were divided into separate piles according to where the dollars went, it would be found that $73 was spent by individuals for medical care; $24 went for local, state, and federal health programs; and the balance was spent by industry and philanthropic institutions and agencies.

Dr. Government One reason for this unprecedented rise in expenditures for medical care has been the increasingly vital role government has assumed in providing the nation with good health care. For example, hundreds of millions of dollars have been spent by the federal government for new and improved hospitals. Thousands of modern, well-equipped hospitals all over the country testify to the success of this aid.

Other government medical expenditures go for public health services, rehabilitation of the disabled, maternal and child health, local and state health programs. Veterans' care represents a major outlay for the federal government, with nearly 114,000 veterans cared for in government hospitals annually.

Research is another major governmental responsibility. In recent years, hundreds of millions of dollars have been spent by the federal government for medical and dental research, much of it by the world-famous National Institutes of Health. Many of the dramatic advances in medicine have resulted from this research. In dentistry, Americans are generally acknowledged to have the best dental care in the world, both in prevention of tooth decay and in repair of damage. Current research promises even greater advances in dental care in the years ahead.

Health insurance The largest percentage increase in total health expenditures since 1950 has been in family outlays for medical and dental care, hospitalization, drugs, and other medical costs. Fortunately, with medical and hospital bills skyrocketing, more and more families have been able to fall back on insurance plans and prepayment programs.

COST OF LIVING AND COST OF MEDICAL CARE

The cost of medical care rose by 127 per cent between 1940 and 1962, compared to a 116 per cent rise in the cost of living.

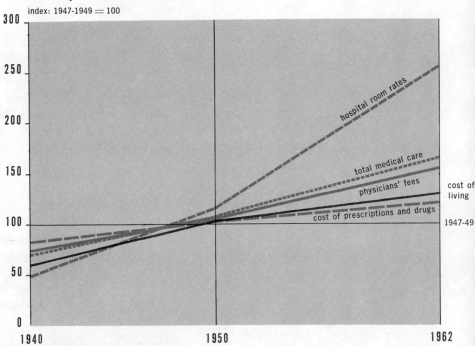

index: 1947-1949 = 100

Individually and in groups, millions of people are covered by such plans. Some use the "Blue Cross" (for hospitalization) and "Blue Shield" (for physicians' and surgeons' bills) plans, both run as nonprofit programs under voluntary community auspices. Others are protected by health and accident policies offered by private insurance companies. And several million individuals and families are enrolled in various prepayment programs under which they obtain protection against medical costs by monthly payments to groups or associations. Many health insurance and prepayment programs are sponsored by employers (including the federal government and some state and local governments) or labor unions. Sometimes there is joint sponsorship.

In 1962, 98 million people were covered by medical care insurance (not including surgery), in contrast to fewer than 22 million in 1950.

About 131 million carried some form of surgical insurance, compared to 54 million in 1950.

And 141 million had hospitalization coverage, a gain of 64 million in 12 years.

HOSPITAL AND MEDICAL INSURANCE, 1962

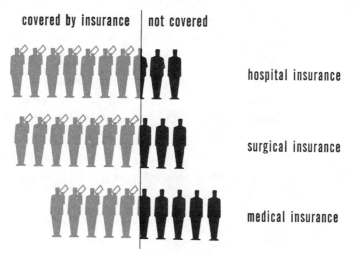

covered by insurance | not covered

hospital insurance

surgical insurance

medical insurance

Each symbol represents 10 per cent of the civilian population.

Such coverage was practically indispensable in the face of rising medical costs. Between 1950 and 1962, total medical care costs rose 56 per cent —more than twice the 26 per cent rise in the cost of living.

Hospital room rates more than doubled in the same period. Physicians' fees increased about 47 per cent. There were also boosts in dentists' and optometrists' fees, drug prices, and other medical expenses normally not covered by insurance. It is not surprising that hospital insurance rates alone more than doubled from 1951 to 1962, just to keep pace with hospital fees.

Fortunately, most Americans (not all) had at least some protection against these sharply rising medical and hospital bills in the early 1960s. Only rarely did they have to borrow heavily or put the family through severe financial sacrifice when illness struck.

Problems to be solved Americans in the 1960s have the benefit of great medical advances. They also are beginning to cope with the costs of illness through various means of financial protection. But there are still basic lacks in the country's medical resources:

Hospital shortage • More hospital beds are needed. In 1945, there were about 13 beds for every 1,000 people; by 1961 the ratio had dropped to about 9 beds

61

per 1,000 people. Many communities are faced with serious shortages of hospital space.

Doctor shortage • The number of physicians is inadequate for the growing population. In 1961, there was an average of 1 physician for every 707 people. In 1900, there was an average of 1 physician for every 636 people. Some states (New York, Massachusetts, California, Connecticut, Colorado, Vermont) have twice as many doctors per 100,000 people as the states at the low end of the income scale (Alabama, Alaska, Mississippi, South Carolina, South Dakota). An increasing number of physicians are choosing research, administration, or other employment—cutting back on the number dedicated to private practice. And many physicians specialize in limited areas of medical care, reducing the number of general practitioners.

Dentist and nurse shortage • More dentists and nurses are needed. There are only about 56 dentists for every 100,000 people. If the nation is to have an adequate dental care program, authorities say this ratio must be increased. The supply of nurses, while it has increased sharply in recent years, is still not equal to the demands made on the nursing profession.

At the present rate of training and population growth, there are expected to be fewer physicians, dentists, and nurses in relation to the total population in 1975 than there were at the beginning of the 1960s. An extensive program of organizing new schools and training facilities seems to be the only way to prevent what could be one of the nation's most serious health problems in the 1970s.

CHAPTER XI

New Look in Education

ACROSS THE LAND a major change has transformed the nation's schools. Part of it is in the structures: gleaming new buildings dot local communities and spruce up hundreds of college campuses. Part of it is in the classrooms: pupils crowd into the classrooms at every level of the school system, often causing even the new buildings to burst at the seams. Part of it is in the teaching staffs and curriculum: the staffs are larger, better trained, and better paid; the curriculum is keyed to a country challenged by the swiftly changing demands of the space age.

Two basic influences have produced this new look in the schools and colleges:

The baby boom, then crowded classrooms ● The "population explosion" of the late 1940s and early 1950s sent a stream of millions of new pupils into the schools, causing overcrowding. first in the elementary schools, later in the high schools and colleges. Now and in the years ahead, this upturn in the birth rate (which continued until 1957) will be felt in every phase of education.

In public elementary schools alone, there has been an enrollment increase of nearly 50 per cent since 1950, when about 19.4 million elementary school and kindergarten pupils were registered. By 1962, about 29 million pupils had to be taken care of.

The postwar baby boom did not begin to affect enrollment in the high schools until the early 1960s. Enrollment in public high schools increased from 5.7 million in 1950 to 10.1 million in 1962, a gain of 77 per cent. High schools will be increasingly crowded in the latter years of the 1960s.

● The fast-paced technological and scientific achievements of the modern world have resulted in urgent demands that America not be left behind in the training and education of her youth. Some people call this the "Sputnik" effect—produced in reaction to public concern over the Russian feat of being first to launch a space satellite.

Thus, the number of high school students taking science courses increased 60 per cent from 1949 to 1959 and the number enrolled in mathematics courses increased 73 per cent. The increases compare with a 45 per cent rise in total enrollment during the same period. At the college level, however, the effect has been less noticeable. Of the 517,000 degrees conferred in 1961-62, more than one fourth were in engineering, mathematics, or the biological, physical, and military sciences—about the same proportion as in 1950.

The price: $32 billion

The price of keeping up with changing demands has been high. In the school year 1962-63, almost $32 billion (including capital outlays) was spent on public and private schools, colleges, universities, and specialized educational institutions. It was more than three times the expenditures of 10 years earlier, over seven times those of 1940. Part of this increase was, of course, due to higher enrollments. But the cost per pupil also soared.

The per pupil cost of operating public schools in 1960 averaged $375, not quite double the 1950 cost. Even when the actual operating expenditures are converted to dollars of constant purchasing power, the rise still amounts to nearly 50 per cent.

SCHOOL OPERATING COSTS PER PUPIL, 1960

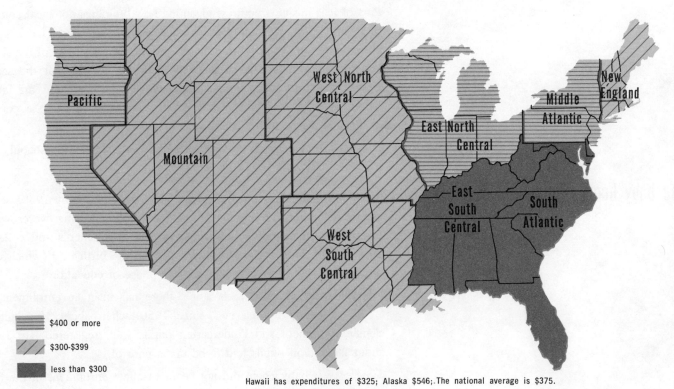

$400 or more

$300-$399

less than $300

Hawaii has expenditures of $325; Alaska $546; The national average is $375.

A more telling measure of how far education has come in the United States is to compare the per pupil cost of school construction and operation today with the $64 spent per pupil in 1920. Even after allowance is made for increases in prices, it is obvious that today's complex world requires far more costly educational facilities than were considered necessary some 40 years ago. In 1960 dollars, the total outlay for school construction and operation per pupil in average daily attendance was five times as much in 1960 as in 1920—$472 compared to $99.

RISE IN COSTS PER PUPIL

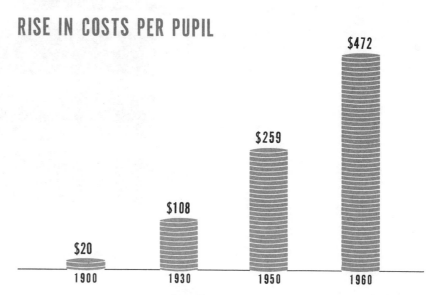

Represents total expenditures (including operation, capital outlay, and interest) per pupil in average daily attendance in public elementary and secondary schools.

For as long as records have been kept, there have been differences in educational expenditures in various sections of the country. Low expenditures reflect mainly low per capita incomes and inability of states and localities to pay for expensive schooling. High expenditures are found in states generally more prosperous than the rest of the nation.

Thus, figured on the number of pupils in average daily attendance, the per pupil expenditure for school operation in Mississippi in 1960 was $206. In New York, it was $562. Per capita personal income in 1960 was $1,168 in Mississippi, $2,778 in New York.

Regional differences are also striking. Highest spending per pupil was in the Middle Atlantic and Pacific states: $496 and $458 per year, respectively. But in the East South Central region (Kentucky, Tennessee, Alabama, Mississippi) average expenditures in 1960 were $232 per pupil.

There are major differences in the amounts spent for education in rural areas and in cities and towns. Almost always, children in rural areas receive poorer schooling. Their teachers receive less pay. They usually have poorer buildings and equipment and go to school fewer days out of the year.

The taxpayer must pay No matter what is spent for public schools, the bills must be met. The financial pressure is greatest at the grass-roots level—in the home towns and counties, which bear nearly three fifths of the expenses for elementary and secondary schools. Public education is the single most important item in most municipal and county budgets. Somewhat less than half the cost is borne by the state governments. The federal government also contributes, but mainly in areas where there are large federal establishments.

In 1910, 63 out of every 100 persons 5 to 19 years of age were in school. By 1960, the number had reached 84 out of every 100.

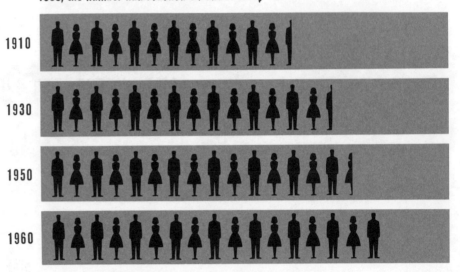

Each symbol represents 5 per cent of all 5-to-19-year-olds.

Three good yardsticks for measuring the quality of the nation's education are:

Going: the little red schoolhouse

● Number of schools. From 1950 to 1960, the number of public elementary schools dropped from 128,000 to 92,000. The drop was largely due to the closing of 40,000 1-room schoolhouses. But there was a net gain of 4,000 multiroom elementary schools and 1,242 high schools. So the country had fewer schools but far more school space.

The intensive building program resulted in the net addition of almost 400,000 classrooms to the nation's public schools between 1954 and 1962. For every 4 new classrooms added 1 classroom was abandoned.

● Number of teachers. In 1963, there were 248,000 more teachers in public elementary schools than there had been in 1953, and 268,000 more in public high schools. The continuing increase in number of teachers has gradually reduced the national average pupil-teacher ratio in public schools—from 31 in elementary schools in 1954 to 29 in 1962. In secondary schools, improvement has been minute—from 21.9 pupils per teacher in 1954 to 21.7 in 1962.

More teachers, better pay

These national averages conceal overcrowding in many schools throughout the country, particularly in large urban areas. In 1962, there were about 915,000 pupils in public elementary schools and 752,000 pupils in public secondary schools enrolled in classes which exceeded "normal capacity." The definition of "normal capacity" varies from state to state and some states have not established a norm. The most common standard is 30 pupils per teacher in grade schools and 25 to 30 pupils per teacher in high schools.

● Teachers' pay. Average salaries of public school teachers rose from $3,405 in 1953 to $5,735 in 1963. High school teachers' pay was higher in 1963—an average of $5,905 per year, compared to $5,560 for elementary school teachers. Despite the obvious effort of the nation to raise its teachers' pay in the quest for good education for its young people, more than one fourth of all teachers were still receiving less

66

than $4,500 a year in 1963. In comparison, the average wage of factory workers in the fall of 1963 was about $5,200 per year.

The private schools Spending for private (including church-connected) elementary and secondary schools has gone up even faster than spending for public schools. It was about 4 times as much in 1961 as it had been 10 years earlier. As in the public schools, there has been rapid expansion of both teaching staffs and number of classrooms. Private schools showed a net increase of 3,200 elementary schools and 730 high schools between 1950 and 1960.

Students who succeed The dropout rate in the high schools is a cause of great national concern. In some areas, it has reached the crisis level. Also confronting educators is the fact that many high school students qualified to go to college do not go, because of either lack of funds or lack of incentive. Nearly all of today's elementary school pupils will probably enter high school, but, if they follow the pattern of recent years, only about two thirds of them will graduate from high school and about one third will enter college.

From the student's point of view, education is the key to good income later in life. The results of a recent survey, reported in the *American Economic Review,* showed that men with only elementary school educations had average lifetime incomes of about $4,700 a year, compared with $6,100 for high school graduates, and $9,500 for college graduates.

HOW MANY PUPILS ARE COLLEGE-BOUND?

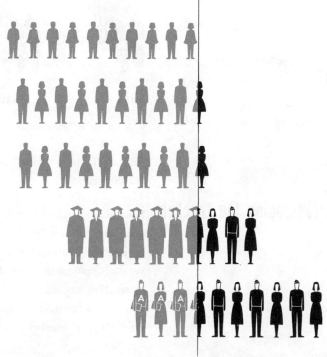

Of 10 students enrolled in fifth grade in 1954:

9.5 went through eighth grade

9.2 went to high school

6.8 graduated from high school

3.4, or half of the high school graduates, went to college in 1962.

College load Despite the dropout rate, more students go on to college today than at any time in the nation's history. This is true in terms both of absolute numbers and of per cent of young people of college age. In 1950, 2.7 million students were enrolled in colleges and universities. By 1962, enrollments for degree credit had soared to 3.8 million—a rise from 30 per cent of all 18-to-21-year-olds in 1950 to 35 per cent in 1962. So rapid an increase was bound to put immense pressure on college facilities.

Colleges and universities are hard-pressed for funds to enlarge faculties and add to facilities. Public and private institutions alike have been forced to increase tuition and other fees to unprecedented levels. About one out of three colleges is supported with public funds; these alone increased expenditures from $1.2 billion in 1950 to $5.1 billion in 1962.

In Western Europe, the general practice is to limit the number enrolled in higher education by means of stiff competitive examinations given at an early age. In the United States, however, the aim is to broaden and enlarge educational opportunities. Enrollments in U.S. colleges and universities are expected to reach at least 6.5 million by 1975.

Junior colleges One solution to the demand for more education has been to encourage expansion and growth of two-year junior colleges. In 1962, there were 564 of these, three fourths of them with fewer than 1,000 students. They seem certain to become increasingly important, particularly in the public education sector.

SPURT IN COLLEGE ENROLLMENT

College enrollment rose 1.7 million from 1940 to 1960. By 1975 it will be 6.5 million, an increase of 3.3 million in 15 years.

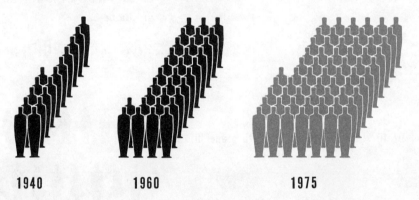

1940   1960   1975

Each full line of figures represents 1 million students enrolled for credit toward a college degree.

Other efforts are also being made to cope with the increasing demands on the schools.

Backstopping the teachers Educational television is now used at all school levels, right up to the graduate schools in the universities. In 1961-62, 6,000 students were registered in educational television courses given by colleges and universities for credit toward degrees.

Successful experiments with teaching machines for instruction in such subjects as languages and sciences point the way to lightening the burden on individual teachers.

"Team" teaching in elementary schools and professor-sharing among groups of colleges are other techniques being tried.

Finally, in order to make maximum use of facilities, the trimester system is spreading to many colleges and universities. Even public elementary and high schools are often used on a year-round basis, partly to lighten the load on overtaxed facilities and partly because of the emphasis on enrichment of the school program with a variety of extracurricular activities, which are often given special attention in summer programs.

The schools begin to integrate

In June 1954, the Supreme Court declared racial segregation in publicly supported schools to be unconstitutional. Almost 10 years later, progress toward integration had been made in many of the states and localities which formerly had had completely segregated schools. But prolonged court actions and local and state resistance, sometimes resulting in federal intervention, marred efforts to achieve a smooth transition in some areas where long-rooted traditions were upset by the Supreme Court ruling. In many communities, even token integration had still not been achieved by the early 1960s. In others, where steps toward school integration had been taken, the problem of school segregation persisted because of segregated housing patterns.

Though progress has been made in improving educational opportunities for the nonwhite population (mostly Negroes) since the Supreme Court decision, the nonwhite population has not caught up with the white population in educational achievement. A few of the lags and also evidences of progress are reflected in these figures:

		white	nonwhite
Per cent enrolled, 1962	7-13 years of age	99.4	98.7
	14-17 years of age	92.7	86.6
Median years of school completed by persons 25 years of age and over	1940	8.7	5.8
	1950	9.7	6.8
	1960	10.9	8.2
Per cent of population 14 years old and over which is illiterate	1947	1.8	11.0
	1959	1.6	7.5

Adults go to school

One of the developments in U.S. education in the 1960s which reflected the growing awareness of the importance of learning was the tremendous growth in adult education. About 3.5 million persons were enrolled in 135,000 special classes offered by public schools outside regular school programs. There were classes in almost everything, from homemaking to business, from physical education to fine arts.

The most popular courses offered training in trade, industrial skills, and technical subjects. Together, they accounted for a sixth of the enrollments in adult classes. Of every 100 adults enrolled, about 13 took courses in homemaking and consumer education, 12 chose academic subjects, and 11 studied business education. Also popular with adults, were arts and crafts, health instruction, physical education, fine arts, and, primarily for new citizens, courses in Americanization and citizenship.

Total expenditures for these special classes in 1959 were $76 million, a fifth of which came from the students themselves.

Reading is also education

Americans have also increased their reading in recent years. The nation's 822 public library systems circulated over 450 million volumes in 1960, almost 100 million more than in 1950. And twice as much was spent for educational books in 1962 as in 1950. Actually, the increase in the number of textbooks purchased was greater than this increased spending indicates, since a growing proportion of the expenditure for textbooks, manuals, and religious books goes for low-priced paperbacks.

Challenge for tomorrow Education is one of America's first domestic concerns for the future. As population grows, schools and colleges must expand. They must be staffed and equipped to train young Americans for positions of leadership in a changing world. In the next 10 years, the demands will be great and the costs monumental. The prospects are that the country will not ignore this need, but, in most areas, will meet it willingly and generously.

CHAPTER XII

America Has Time for Fun

WHEN THE NATION WAS YOUNG, no one was likely to worry about what to do in his spare time. Life was an early-to-rise, early-to-bed routine. There were few idle hours, except on Sunday, and that was a day given to worship.

How all that has changed!

Nowadays, it is considered important for children and young people to have time for fun as well as for work. Housewives have been provided with labor-saving devices to free them from much household drudgery. Family breadwinners have more time than ever to call their own.

All that spare time Today's worker has an average of about 25 more free hours per week than did the worker of a century ago. His life is compounded of time on the job and time off the job—the job usually consuming 40 hours in a 5-day week, and the time off the job consisting of time before and after work, weekends, holidays, and annual vacations.

Having this free time is a welcome boon to most. It means rest, relaxation, and a chance to take care of household chores. Or it may be used to work at a second job. But, not surprisingly, the prospect that the nation may be moving into an era of an even shorter work week disturbs many people.

Even today, the challenge of how to use leisure hours effectively is a serious one. Many complain of lack of time to do all the things they want to get done in the hours not consumed by the job.

71

So many things to do

Americans of all ages have endless uses for their spare time—the car to travel in; the TV set to watch; hobbies to pursue; parks to play in, picnic in, camp in; oceans, rivers, streams, and pools to swim in, boat on, water ski on; ball games to watch or play; gardens to cultivate; walking and hiking to do; musical instruments to play; records to listen to; movies, concerts, and plays to attend; indoor and outdoor games to enjoy; books and magazines to read. And many of these activities can be—and are —carried on while listening to the radio.

Then there are family and community responsibilities. When adult Americans aren't using their so-called "leisure time" for shopping, commuting, or running errands, they may be involved in "do-it-yourself" projects around the house, practicing "togetherness" with their families, or performing some community service, such as leading a troop of Boy Scouts or handling a PTA assignment.

The recreation bill goes up and up

Feeding the market for recreational goods and services is a multibillion-dollar assortment of businesses, which do everything from supplying the golf clubs for weekend golfers to repairing television sets, operating theaters and making children's toys. In 1962, American consumers spent $19 billion for recreational activities and equipment, almost double the 1950 figure. But prices were higher in 1962 and the population was larger. In 1960 dollars the increase was only 53 per cent. And there were millions of additional pleasure-seekers contributing to recreation expenditures.

Recreational spending per person in 1962 averaged about $101—almost 25 per cent more than in 1950 (in 1960 dollars). Of every dollar spent by consumers, an average of about five and a half cents—an all-time high—went for recreation in 1962.

Local, state, and federal governments spent another billion dollars equipping, staffing, and maintaining beaches, picnic areas, and other public recreational facilities.

If there is added to this the money spent on vacation travel—estimated to run as high as $20 billion a year—it seems pretty clear that close to $40 billion a year was spent on all phases of recreation in 1962.

CONSUMER SPENDING FOR RECREATION

In dollars, spending for recreation rose $9 billion between 1950 and 1962—an increase of 90 per cent.

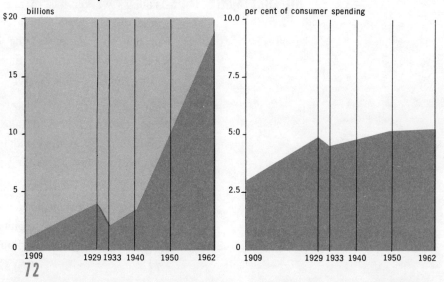

But the movie bill goes down While spending for most recreational activities has gone up since 1950, there are some significant exceptions. The most striking has been in spending for the movies. In dollars of constant value, this declined by 29 per cent between 1950 and 1962.

In the depression year of 1933, an average of about 26 cents of every dollar spent on recreation went for movie tickets. But in 1962, only 7.5 cents of every recreation dollar went to movie box offices. The all-time high for the movies' share was in 1943—30 cents. Movie attendance records reveal a similar trend: from 1935 to 1948 movie attendance was high—an average of 80 to 90 million persons per week, or over 60 per cent of the population. Attendance began to decline in 1949, and by 1962 was down to 42 million a week—23 per cent of the population.

Plays and operas Spending for plays and operas (never, of course, as popular as motion pictures) has not followed the same pattern as spending for the movies. It increased about 58 per cent (in constant dollars) between 1950 and 1960.

Television Television seems to have been the main reason for the more than decade-long drop in movie attendance. But average daily hours of viewing per person apparently reached a peak in the mid-1950s and by 1962 TV's magic had somewhat dimmed. And the movie business was showing signs of a modest pickup.

Television has also affected attendance at sports events. Many people would rather watch games on television than go to see them. Total expenditures for spectator sports (in constant dollars) declined by 9 per cent between 1950 and 1960. A smaller share of the recreation dollar—one and a half cents—was spent for admissions to sports events in 1962 than at any other time since 1941, when the share was almost 3 cents.

Still, 40 million people attended major league baseball and college football games in 1962, compared to not quite 37 million in 1950—when the nation was smaller. One sport which has greatly increased in popularity is horse racing. In 1962, almost 50 million people attended the races, 70 per cent more than in 1950.

The favorite sports What about participant sports—the kind people engage in themselves? Here, the story is different. Of every dollar spent on recreation in 1950, seven cents went for such activities. By 1962, the figure was nine cents.

Practically every sport reflected this urge of Americans to get out and play. Compared to 1950, by 1961 there were:

- At least 50 per cent more bowlers and golfers.
- More than three times as many softball players, skiers, and boaters.
- At least a third more basketball, football, and table tennis players.

Let's swim! Of all outdoor activities, water sports have had the most dramatic growth. There were eight times as many swimming pools in 1960 as there had been just after World War II. Five million people have taken up skin and scuba diving. The number of boats sold annually has just about doubled since 1950. An estimated 6.25 million outboard motors were in use in 1962. Swimming and water skiing have reached new heights of popularity—with an estimated 33 million swimmers and over 5 million water skiers in the early 1960s.

Bowling, boating, fishing, and swimming are the most popular sports—each with 30 or 40 million participants. The "physical fitness" program urged on Americans by their government officials and doctors has obviously been taken quite seriously.

CHANGES IN CONSUMER RECREATIONAL SPENDING

A significant trend is the increasing emphasis on active sports and sports equipment.

per cent of total recreational expenditures

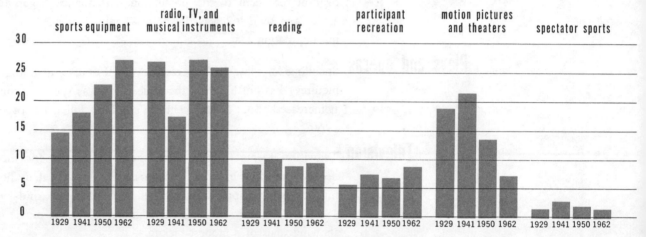

With this kind of interest, spending has soared on such items as tennis rackets, golf clubs, baseball gloves, boats, etc. It increased over 75 per cent (in constant dollars) in a decade. Sports equipment and toys together now take the largest share of the recreation dollar—about 27 per cent, compared with 23 per cent in 1950.

Hobbies by the dozen Millions of people have plunged wholeheartedly into an assortment of other activities and hobbies. Between 1950 and 1962, for example, here is how spending (in constant dollars) increased for a few of them:

 reading for pleasure, 64 per cent

 photography and stamp and coin collecting, 87 per cent

 gardening, 71 per cent

 radio, TV, records, and musical instruments, 61 per cent

 club activities, 18 per cent

What do people enjoy doing the most? A report to the President in 1962 by the Outdoor Recreation Resources Review Commission said that the most popular outdoor activities are pleasure driving and walking. These two alone account for about 42 per cent of outdoor activity.

Family holiday Over half of U. S. families took at least one vacation trip in 1961. Ninety per cent of all pleasure and vacation travel is done by car. Vacationers drove a total of almost 70 billion miles in 1961 and they spent an estimated $20 billion.

Wherever they headed, vacationers were apt to encounter crowded and often costly facilities. While America has plenty of park and recreational space, much of it is located far from population centers.

Parks and people Particularly is this true of national parks and recreation areas in national forests and wilderness areas. There were 234 million acres in public outdoor recreation areas—federal, state, and local—in the early 1960s. But, nationally at least (to quote the Outdoor Recreation Resources Review Commission), "these recreation areas are located where the people are not."

Only 15 per cent of the people live in the West—where most of the parks are. And over a quarter of the nation's population is in the crowded Northeast—where national parks are practically nonexistent. The result is that the approximately two out of three people who live in the great metropolitan areas are not within easy driving distance of the nation's parks and forests.

Nevertheless, there is no lack of visitors to these areas. In 1955, there were about 56 million visits to the national parks. Seven years later, there were 87 million visits to these parks—an increase of 4.5 million a year. No wonder the parks have trouble coping with the crowds!

Visits to the national forests more than doubled in the same period—from 46 million to 113 million.

In the state parks, which have become more numerous in recent years, the number of visits has been mounting at a spectacular rate of about 15 million per year—to almost 275 million in 1961.

FAVORITE OUTDOOR RECREATION

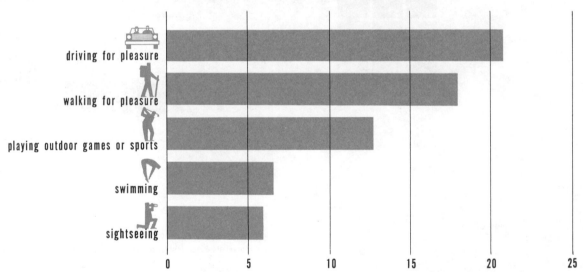

Length of bar indicates average number of days each person 12 years of age and over engaged in activity, June 1, 1960-May 30, 1961.

Disappearing seashore Should the vacationing family turn to the seashore instead of the parks, it again would find the crowds getting bigger. One reason is lack of public shoreline for recreation. Of the 60,000 miles of ocean and Great Lakes shoreline, only a third is suitable for development for recreation. But less than 2 per cent of the total shoreline (336 miles on the Atlantic Coast and 296 miles on the Pacific Coast, for example) is in public ownership. Disappearing shoreline for public use has reached almost a critical point.

Play space in home towns Many towns and cities have tried hard to provide their residents with more play space. The result: over the past 10 years or so, there has been a doubling of baseball diamonds and recreation centers, an increase of almost 25 per cent in the number of outdoor playgrounds, and a significant growth in such facilities as golf courses, recreation

75

buildings, stadiums, swimming pools, tennis courts. Thousands more paid recreation leaders have been hired, and the number of volunteer leaders in various types of community recreational activities has more than tripled.

How well are cities meeting their recreational needs? One measure is the amount of money being spent. The National Recreation Association specifies that—aside from equipment and buildings—a municipality should spend a minimum of $6 annually per resident for operating, maintaining, and staffing recreational facilities. Only about one out of six cities surveyed in 1960 reported meeting or exceeding this minimum.

RECREATION AREAS AND POPULATION, 1960

Major parks and national forests are distant from the nation's population centers.

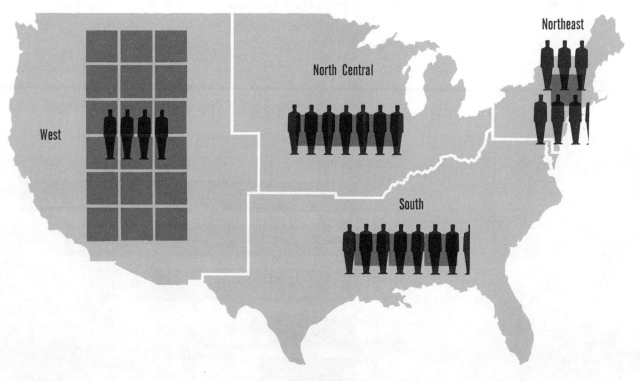

Each person represents 4 per cent of population of the 48 contiguous states.
Each square represents 4 per cent of nonurban public recreation areas in the 48 contiguous states.

It is apparent that the nation faces a challenge in planning proper use of its leisure time. It also faces an urgent need to create adequate facilities for outdoor recreation in parks and play areas. The challenge and the need will require an increasing amount of attention from everyone in both the near and far future.

CHAPTER XIII

GOING PLACES

THE UNITED STATES is a nation on the move. Never have Americans been able to travel so fast. Never have they been able to go so far with such ease. On the ground and in the air, a transport revolution has changed the face of the nation. It has brought the West Coast and East Coast within five hours of each other. And it has shrunk the globe to the point where distance is no longer a barrier to the traveler.

Astonishing as the results of this revolution appear, its achievement has been accompanied by a multitude of problems. Some are familiar, such as looking for a parking space on a crowded downtown street. Some are ambitious and challenging, such as perfecting a 1,500-mile-per-hour airplane.

Nation on the move

The upheaval in U. S. transportation began years ago and shows no sign of abating. Its beginnings can be traced to the period when the automobile emerged from the status of a rich man's toy to the common man's basic form of transportation.

One of the most striking phases of the revolution came after World War II, when the number of automobiles and buses—both in cities and on the highways—skyrocketed. Simultaneously, airplanes emerged as a fast, efficient, and relatively economical means of long-distance travel, and railroads struggled to hold on to a disappearing patronage.

Box Score: 1940-1962

Between 1940 and 1962:

- The number of privately owned passenger cars rose from 27 million to about 66 million.

77

● Plane passengers increased from about 2.5 million to about 60 million annually.

● Bus passengers increased from 140 million per year to almost twice that number.

● Train passengers dropped from about 456 million to 313 million annually.

● Privately owned motor truck registrations went from 4.6 million to 12.2 million.

The figures speak for themselves: Americans were traveling less by train, more by car, bus, and plane. And they were depending more on trucks for shipments of freight and express.

HOW AMERICANS TRAVELED IN 1962

passenger miles, billions

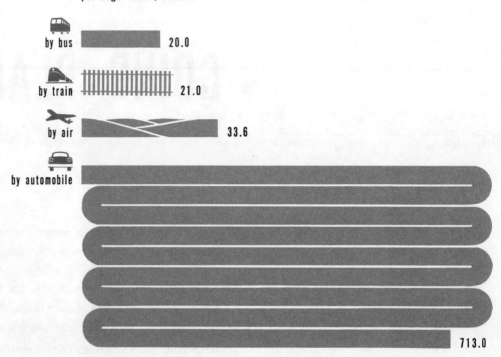

by bus — 20.0

by train — 21.0

by air — 33.6

by automobile — 713.0

Local public carriers and inland waterways not included.

Fading glory of the railroads

As recently as 1929, the chances were four to one that anyone traveling from one city to another would go by rail. Even in 1950, about half of all travel on public carriers was by train. But by 1962, almost as many people were traveling by bus as by train. And for long-distance travel, people turned increasingly to airplanes; that year, domestic plane travel (measured in passenger-miles) exceeded train travel by more than 50 per cent. The total volume of domestic air passenger traffic in 1962 was close to 35 billion passenger-miles.

Ten miles a minute in a jet

The ten-mile-a-minute jet is a phenomenon of the sixties. It has revolutionized overseas travel and has put all major cities in the nation within a few hours of each other. One measure of the importance of jets in the transport system is the amount of fuel they consume. In 1955, they used only 2 million gallons of jet fuel, compared with 912 million gallons of gasoline used in propeller flights. Six years later, on domestic flights alone, jets were burning up 1.5 billion gallons of fuel a year. At least another half billion gallons of fuel were used by U. S. jets in international flights. Use of gasoline in domestic propeller flights had declined to 774 million gallons per year.

King automobile Dramatic as are the swift jets, the true king of U. S. transportation in the sixties is the automobile. In 1962, Americans drove their cars more than 700 billion miles—nearly 10 times the combined distance covered by trains, buses, and planes. In the early 1960s they bought about 6 million cars a year, but in some years sales exceeded 7 million. The rate of increase in car ownership has been more than three and a half times the rate of increase in the nation's population, and almost twice the growth rate of the country's economy.

The entire U. S. population could get into these cars simultaneously (a forbidding thought), and there would be more than enough room for everyone. In 1962, there was 1 car registered for each 2.8 people. In 1930, the ratio was one car for every five people. Here are some other facts about cars that contribute to America's reputation as a "nation on wheels":

The soaring statistics of car ownership • Four out of five families now own cars. And more than one out of every five families boasts two or more cars in the garage.

• Car ownership is highest in relation to population in the West and North Central states. California leads in total registrations—6.9 million in 1961. Next in order of car registration that year came New York, Pennsylvania, Ohio, Texas, Illinois, Michigan, New Jersey, Florida, Indiana.

THE SHIFT FROM THE RAILROADS

In 1962, less than 3 per cent of passenger travel was by train. Only 46 years earlier almost three fourths of all travel was by train.

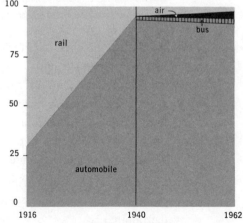
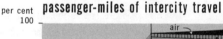
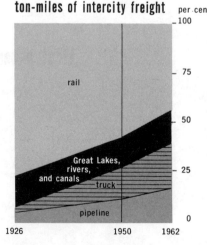

Inland waterways and local public carriers not included.   Air carriers not included.

• Because of the availability of mass transit facilities (and perhaps also because traffic congestion and parking problems make driving uncomfortable and inconvenient) people in cities of 500,000 or more are less likely to own cars than people in smaller communities. In small cities, 3 out of 4 families are car owners, compared with 6 out of 10 in big cities. In suburban areas, however, nearly 9 out of 10 families have at least one car.

● The richer one gets, the more likely he is to own an automobile. The chances that a family with an income under $4,000 a year will have a car are about 50-50. But in families with incomes over $10,000 a year, car ownership is practically 100 per cent. Two of every five families in this income bracket have at least two cars.

There is one other notable fact about the United States and its love affair with the automobile: increasingly it shares this love with other countries. In 1940, about 74 per cent of the world's cars were owned by Americans; 20 years later, the U. S. share was down to 63 per cent.

CAR REGISTRATION AND POPULATION GROWTH

The increase in the nation's cars is at a much faster rate than population growth.

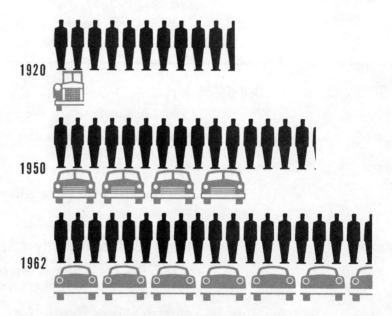

1920

1950

1962

Each man symbol represents 10 million people.

Each car symbol represents 10 million registered privately owned passenger cars.

What a car is used for Americans use their cars for everything: shopping, business, commuting, pleasure. A glance into any shopping center parking lot will illustrate how vital the car is to shopping. As for commuting, in the last 30 years rail commuters have dropped off about one third; bus and trolley lines serving commuters have lost at least 50 per cent of their customers since 1945. But there is more commuting today, not less, and it is the automobile which commuters increasingly depend on.

One fifth of all motor trips are for pleasure—social and recreational purposes and vacations. Nine out of ten families take their vacations in the family car.

Overseas travelers Just as the car is used on U. S. streets and highways for work and pleasure, ships and planes carry Americans on overseas trips. Nearly 1.8 million Americans went abroad (exclusive of Canada and Mexico) in 1962, two and a half times the number who went in 1950. In 1950, about 45 per cent of overseas travelers went by boat. In 1962, four out of five went by plane—mainly jet. But more than 200,000 Europe-bound travelers that year still preferred to go by ship.

80

FOREIGN TRAVEL IS BIG BUSINESS

American tourists spent almost $2 billion for foreign travel in 1962.

Each symbol equals $100 million spent by American travelers abroad in 1962.

Changing freight patterns The means of transport used for shipping goods—raw materials and finished products—has also changed over the years. About 35 years ago, over three quarters of all freight shipments went by rail. An estimated 16 per cent moved by boat on the inland waterways. Trucks and pipelines took the rest.

By 1962, the picture had changed. The railroads' portion of intercity freight had dropped to less than 45 per cent. Trucks carried about 23 per cent of the total. Oil and gas pipelines snaked their way into every industrial center, and were responsible for nearly 18 per cent of all domestic freight shipments. Shipments by inland waterways were still holding their own, with about 16 per cent of the total. Coming up rapidly—though still of only negligible importance—was air freight. Air freight shipments were only one six-hundredth of shipments transported by train.

More roads, more airports The superpowered automobile has brought a new look to the city and countryside, with a web of highways crisscrossing the nation. In a decade, over 600,000 miles of paved roads were added to the national highway system. Some were two-lane roads for farm-to-market travel. Some served the dynamic complex of suburban communities. But the greatest miracle wrought by the bulldozers and earth movers was a spreading system of national superhighways, built to cope with the millions of new cars that demanded space to move in. By 1961, the national interstate highway system stretched 41,000 miles.

Airplanes—especially the jets—also generated basic changes in the national transportation picture. Between 1950 and 1960, air routes more than doubled—from 70,000 to a total of 179,000 miles. This expansion called for more airports, and 312 new ones were opened. It also required elaborate new electronic traffic controls, very high frequency communications systems, and an advanced navigation system, which in another year or two will alter significantly present methods of plane routing and control.

The coming transport crisis

In some ways, the nation is only beginning to sense its transportation problems of tomorrow. It is a rare community that won't soon have to wrestle—if it is not already wrestling—with the need to provide more parking space for its shoppers and commuters. Traffic control will become increasingly complicated, as cars compete for driving room. Though there are 430,000 miles of freeways, parkways, and streets in the nation's cities, motorists even now often move only at a snail's pace.

Many cities — for example, Boston, San Francisco, and Washington — regard rail transit as the main solution to their transportation problems. They believe the need is to persuade people to move by train, subway, or monorail and leave their cars at home. If this theory works, it could mean a turnaround in the status of trains as major passenger carriers.

In the air, helicopters and other forms of vertical take-off-and-landing planes are considered indispensable for the future. Three helicopter lines—in Los Angeles, Chicago, and New York—already carry some half million passengers a year. Meanwhile, by the 1970s, planes flying at twice the speed of sound will be routine, bringing with them a whole new set of critical problems of routing and control.

The greatest challenge facing the planners will be on the superhighways. It is estimated that by 1975 at least 100 million cars will be in use by a population more car-conscious than ever. Building highways for these cars and maintaining adequate safety measures will get priority attention from every state and community. The coming crisis in the automobile age will test to the limit the resources and skills of the nation's traffic experts.

CHAPTER XIV

Government of the People

NO MATTER WHERE ONE LOOKS, he can see—and feel—the long arm of government. Government is the post office on the green and the policeman on the corner. It is the launch site at Cape Kennedy and the global communications center in the Pentagon. It is the school down the street and the busy west wing of the nation's White House. There are few, if any, areas of living in the United States in the 1960s that are not affected by government in one way or another.

Government: the biggest "business"

Government has been expanding faster than any other sector of the economy, and today the "business" of government is the country's largest and most influential activity. A total of $161 billion was spent in 1962 by local, state, and federal governments for compensation of employees, purchases of goods and services, transfer payments (such as social security and veterans' benefits), interest, and other outlays.

The $161 billion was an all-time high in net government expenditures. Thirty years previously—in 1932—total spending by government was only about $11 billion. Even at the peak of World War II, when federal spending shot upward, total expenditures were a little more than $100 billion. Since the mid-1950s, spending has been rising steadily. Year by year, increases during this period ranged from $5 billion to more than $14 billion.

There is no question that the responsibilities of government are greater now than they were a generation ago. For one thing, there were about 62 million more people in 1962 than there were 30 years earlier. Even so, the cost of government per person today —about $950—is far higher than it was in 1932—about $100. In 1960 dollars the figures are $911 and $317, respectively.

Obviously, then, government is doing more now than it did a generation ago. This is true both of local and state governments and of the federal government—though it is the federal treasury which has been the major source of the mounting expenditures. In 1932, the amount of money spent by local and state governments was more than double the federal outlays. Today, the federal government spends about $1.74, excluding grants-in-aid to state and local governments, for every $1 spent at the state and local levels.

Another way of measuring the shift is this: in the last 30 years or so, federal spending has multiplied 34 times, state and local spending 8 times. The national government today plays a far more important role in the average citizen's welfare and security than ever before in the nation's history.

GROWTH OF DIRECT GOVERNMENT EXPENDITURES

Federal expenditures have been increasing faster than state and local government spending. Defense needs currently represent about half of the federal budget.

TOTAL DIRECT
GOVERNMENT
EXPENDITURES

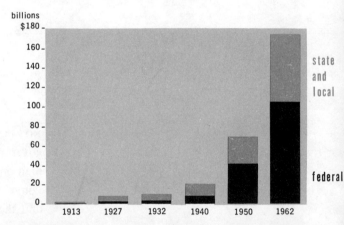

SELECTED MAJOR DIRECT GOVERNMENT EXPENDITURES

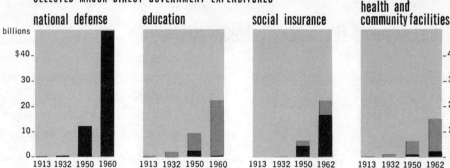

 Effect of inflation While the needs have multiplied, the ever-rising cost of government cannot be blamed exclusively on the spread of the activities of government. Just as the family must pay more now than a generation ago for comparable goods and services, government also feels the bite of inflation. If there had been no rises in prices in the past 30 years, federal expenditures in 1962 would have been only about 10 times as high as in 1932, not 34 times. And state and local expenditures would have been about two and a half times as high, not eight times.

Federal spending Essentially, it was spending for defense and public welfare which propelled federal expenditures to the 1962 level of nearly $110 billion.

The cold war, international tensions, fantastic costs of modern armaments and weapons, and military commitments at innumerable spots around the globe have combined to make national defense extremely costly. Today, roughly 50 cents out of every dollar spent by the federal government goes for current defense purposes.

Related and comparatively recent expenditures are for the space program and scientific research. Just as the schools are putting heavy emphasis on the sciences, the government is spending billions of dollars on research, scientific studies, and technological undertakings, particularly in relation to the rocket and space efforts. About a ninth of all federal spending goes for these purposes.

Another sixth of federal expenditures goes for social security and public assistance programs. More than ever before, the federal government, aided by state and local administrations, is involved in programs connected with the welfare of individual citizens.

The cost of helping the nation's farmers and improving agricultural and other natural resources has risen steadily in recent years. In 1950, the federal government spent not quite $4 billion for these purposes. Eleven years later—in 1961—the price tag for these outlays was over $10 billion. This was approximately 10 cents out of every dollar spent by the federal treasury.

Another major federal outlay is for interest on the national debt ($256 billion at the end of 1962). About $1 out of $13 of the federal budget went for interest on this debt in 1962. In 1950, with a debt of $219 billion, interest payments represented $1 out of $7 of all federal spending.

Where state and local taxes go Changing needs have also affected state and local budgets, but not quite so dramatically as they have affected the federal budget. State and local governments have always found their major costs were for education, roads, health, and community facilities. These responsibilities have become increasingly important in recent years.

In 1962, for example, they accounted for nearly $2 out of $3 spent by state and local governments. Education represented 31 per cent of the total; highways, 15 per cent; health and community facilities, 18 per cent.

What government provides The combined expenditures at all levels of government make possible the network of government activities which bind the nation together, maintain its welfare and security, and provide a stable environment for economic growth. Included among these activities—to name a few at random—are operating the postal service, building and maintaining highways, regulating communications and transportation, creating water and power facilities, providing adequate fire and police protection, establishing recreational areas, building public housing, regulating banks and other financial institutions, supervising foreign relations, supplying veterans' benefits.

Where does the money come from to pay the bill for all this? About $3 out of $4 come from the citizen's purse in the form of taxes. The rest is borrowed, or is collected by government as fees and payments for the services it performs.

Where the money comes from Some is transferred from one level of government to provide money to another level—the federal government makes grants to the states and states allocate funds to towns and cities, for example. These intergovernmental transfers do not affect the total government expenditures. But they do make it possible for certain activities—education and social security programs, for instance—to be provided on a uniform minimum basis for all the nation's citizens. In 1962, local governments received 25 per cent of their revenues from state and federal sources. The federal government provided 19 per cent of state revenues. Federal aid to state and local governments accounted for 11 per cent of their combined revenues in 1962.

GOVERNMENT RECEIPTS, 1962

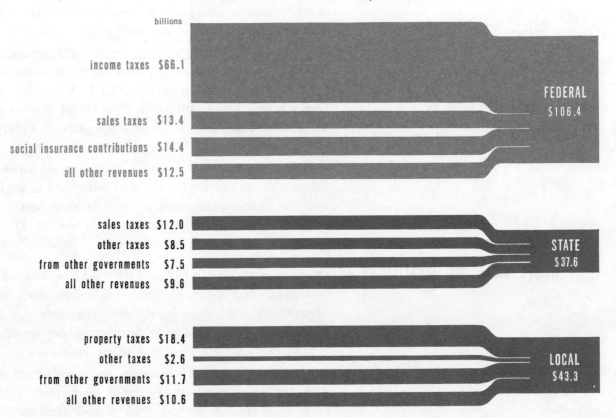

billions

income taxes $66.1

sales taxes $13.4

social insurance contributions $14.4

all other revenues $12.5

FEDERAL $106.4

sales taxes $12.0

other taxes $8.5

from other governments $7.5

all other revenues $9.6

STATE $37.6

property taxes $18.4

other taxes $2.6

from other governments $11.7

all other revenues $10.6

LOCAL $43.3

No matter how the pie is cut, most of the bill must be paid by the nation's taxpayers.

They pay an overwhelming amount of it in three different forms: income taxes (paid by 61 million individual taxpayers and 1.1 million corporate taxpayers in 1960), sales taxes, and property taxes. Other types of levies, such as taxes on cigarettes and gasoline and duties on imported goods, are less important in terms of total revenue produced.

The federal government relies mainly on income taxes. State governments get most of their funds from retail sales taxes. Growing numbers of states also levy income taxes. The traditional source of most local revenue has been the property tax, but local governments are turning increasingly to sales taxes for additional revenue.

The tax bill: $682 per person

In 1962, these and other taxes provided local, state, and federal governments with a revenue of $127 billion—more than one fifth of the total gross national product. Taxes amounted to about $682 per person—two thirds of which went to the federal treasury and the rest to local and state treasuries. And they were more than 10 times the average taxes per person in 1932. In dollars of equal purchasing power, 1962 taxes per person were five times higher than the 1932 taxes.

Government as an employer

What happens to the taxes one pays? Most go to pay salaries of government workers and to cover costs of the goods and services government purchases.

One out of seven employed civilians had a job at some level of government in 1962. About 7 million of them worked for state and local governments, more than two and one half times the number employed in 1932. The rest—2.5 million—were employed by federal agencies. This was more than four times the number working for the federal government in 1932.

Defense was the biggest employer in the federal government (43 employees out of every 100). The Post Office had nearly 600,000 workers and the Department of Agriculture accounted for more than 100,000 federal jobs in 1962. The majority of government jobs at the local level were in education.

In 1962, the average pay check for all civilian and military government workers, federal, state, and local, was slightly above $5,000 a year.

GOVERNMENT AS AN EMPLOYER

One out of seven employed civilians worked for government in 1962.

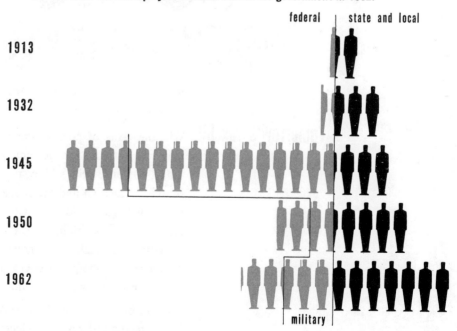

Each symbol represents 1 million government employees.

Government, the biggest customer

Just as government is the nation's biggest employer, it is also industry's biggest customer. All governing units combined—federal, state, county, town, municipality, school district, and other special districts—totaled 91,236 in 1962. Each of these must buy services and supplies, ranging from a multimillion-dollar expenditure for a rocket program to a few hundred dollars for new benches in the town square.

These purchases of goods and services came to $117 billion in 1962. They accounted for $1 out of every $5 of the nation's business. The federal government spent $62 billion of the total (85 per cent of it for defense activities); state and local governments, $55 billion.

The importance of government purchases in the economy is pointed up by the change since 1929, when total government purchases came to only $8.5 billion, a mere 8 per cent of the nation's GNP. Government purchases in 1962 were 21 per cent of GNP.

GOVERNMENT EXPENDITURES AS PER CENT OF GNP

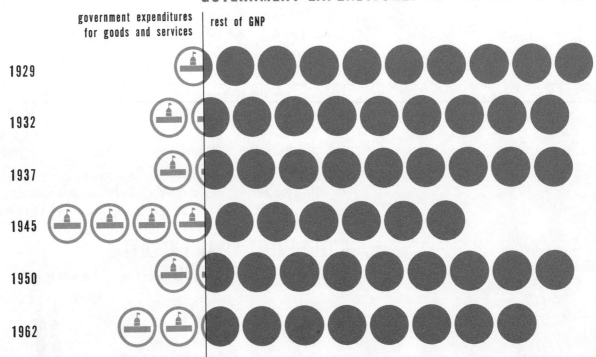

government expenditures for goods and services | rest of GNP

1929
1932
1937
1945
1950
1962

Each symbol represents 10 per cent of GNP.

Tomorrow's tax bill Will the costs of government decline in the future? The prospects are they will not, and for the same reasons which keep costs and taxes high today. Defense will still command a huge portion of the nation's resources. Research and the space program will undoubtedly expand. The nation will grow and with it the need for social insurance, welfare programs, transportation, education, municipal services, and the other activities undertaken by government for its citizens. It is probable, therefore, that the government share of the nation's gross national product will not be lower than what it is now.

The tax bills from local and state governments are likely to mount. The bill from the federal tax collector may be reduced somewhat. While the total tax bill may increase, the nation's ability to pay taxes will probably be greater, thanks to a vigorous and expanding economy.

CHAPTER XV

The People's Welfare

NOT SO LONG AGO, the average worker did not have much to fall back on when he became ill or lost his job or found that he had reached an age when no one wanted to hire him. If he was lucky, he had savings to see him through the crisis. Otherwise, he depended on family or friends or, in the most desperate situations, on private or public charity.

Private welfare no longer the mainstay

He was less fortunate than some of his Western European cousins, who, as far back as the last century, had unemployment insurance, health insurance, old-age pensions, and other protective measures against whatever misfortunes might befall them. In the United States, social insurance programs grew out of the depression of the 1930s, as did many of the Western European programs. However, social insurance in Western Europe is generally older and broader in scope than in the United States.

Over the past 30 years, a marked change has taken place in the U.S. approach to the problem of the individual's welfare and security. Privately supported welfare plans and philanthropy are no longer the mainstay of the family in distress. They are still important, but they play a secondary role to the government-sponsored and government-administered social insurance and public aid programs. Annual expenditures for public (government-run) welfare programs in 1961 were fully six times as much as expenditures for private welfare programs.

Government social insurance

The government social insurance plans—federal, state, and local—take care of many of the elderly and disabled. They protect against unemployment and the loss of family breadwinners. They assure income for orphans and widows of insured workers. Special programs cover veterans, railroad workers, and government employees.

GROWTH OF WELFARE EXPENDITURES

Though expenditures for private welfare in 1961 were more than four times 1930 expenditures, they were only 14 per cent of total expenditures for welfare in 1961, compared with about one half in 1930.

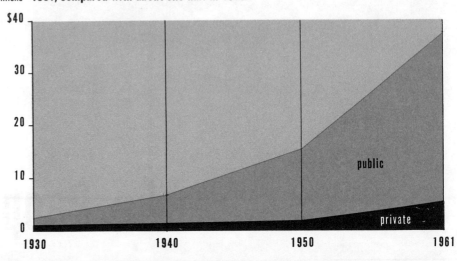

billions

Public aid programs Under various public aid programs, federal, state, and local governments also assist the old and infirm who have no other means of support; the blind and otherwise handicapped; dependent children; and destitute families cut off from all other sources of income.

Public welfare benefits: $32.5 billion Altogether, the cost of benefits paid under these programs—social insurance and public aid—at all levels of government, came to $32.5 billion in 1962. This was more than two and a quarter times the $14.3 billion spent in 1950, and 32 times as much as was spent for public welfare in 1930, when public welfare programs consisted primarily of local relief, veterans' pensions and insurance, and government employee retirement programs. In constant dollars, 1962 expenditures were about twice 1950 expenditures and 18 times the amount spent in 1930. The $32.5 billion spent by government in 1962 was partly offset by contributions of both employees and employers to the federal old-age and survivors insurance program and of employers to the federal-state unemployment insurance program.

The beneficiaries Here are how the five major groups of beneficiaries of the nation's public welfare programs have benefited in recent years:

● The retired—There were 13 million people, most of them past the retirement age, receiving social security or other public retirement benefits in 1962. Their average benefit was $77 a month or $925 a year. Altogether, about a billion dollars a month was paid out to these individuals by various government agencies. There were also 2 million individuals under private pension and profit-sharing arrangements, receiving an average of $1,000 a year in benefits, over and above what they may have been receiving from government programs.

● The survivors—In 1961, there were about 6 million of these—widows, widowers, dependent children (under 18), or parents—survivors of

PEOPLE HELPED BY WELFARE PROGRAMS, 1961

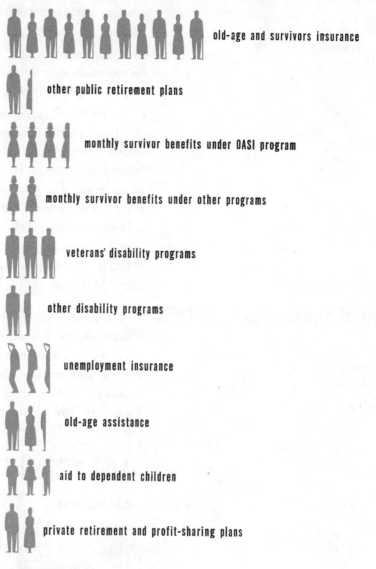

old-age and survivors insurance

other public retirement plans

monthly survivor benefits under OASI program

monthly survivor benefits under other programs

veterans' disability programs

other disability programs

unemployment insurance

old-age assistance

aid to dependent children

private retirement and profit-sharing plans

Each symbol represents 1 million persons.

deceased workers covered by social security. They received an average of $57 a month, bringing the total government expenditure for this purpose to $4.1 billion in that year. Survivors also receive a lump-sum benefit at the time of the breadwinner's death. In 1961, about $171 million was paid out to 816,000 survivors in lump-sum payments, an average of about $210 per beneficiary.

Excluding railroad and government employees, about 56 million workers had old-age and survivors insurance coverage in 1962.

● The ill—In 1961, about 4.5 million people who were too ill or disabled to work received a total of $5.5 billion, or an average of $100 a month per person, in benefits under government disability programs. In addition, private health insurance plans (including sick benefit provisions in some cases) covered a total of nearly 137 million people. These plans paid out $3.4 billion in that year. Nearly $900 million of this represented payments for loss of income due to illness.

● The unemployed—Unemployment in recent years has been running at between 5 and 6 per cent of the total work force. Millions of the jobless are entitled to unemployment benefits, either through state-federal coverage or through special programs for railroad workers and veterans. In 1962, $3.1 billion was paid out to 1.8 million unemployed. Average weekly payments were about $35, and continued for an average of about 13 weeks.

In 1950, unemployment benefits averaged only $21 a week. The gain isn't as much as it seems, however. In 1950's purchasing power, 1962's $35 was worth only $28.

● The needy—Government still spends billions of dollars in direct benefits to people not covered by social insurance. These include dependent children, the aged, the blind and disabled, the destitute ill, and families in need of public relief. In 1962, $4.5 billion was spent for these purposes, most of it going to about 2.3 million old people and nearly 3 million dependent children. A generation ago, all those in need of public aid had only local relief agencies to turn to. These had a caseload of more than 1 million in 1936. Thanks to improved economic conditions and federally assisted public aid and social insurance programs, there were only 353,000 people on local relief rolls in 1962.

Cost of private welfare: $5 billion

Cost of private welfare programs in 1961 came to $5.3 billion, two and a half times the amount spent in 1950. Of the total, $1.8 billion, or one third, was paid in benefits to employees covered by private health, welfare, and pension plans. The rest—$3.5 billion—represented contributions by Americans to private charities. Whereas in 1930, contributions to private charities accounted for over a third of all welfare expenditures, 31 years later they were only 8 per cent of the total.

MAJOR WELFARE EXPENDITURES

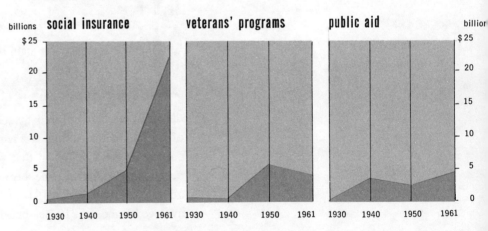

It has been estimated that about three out of four dollars received by the private charities in recent years came out of individuals' pockets. The fourth dollar was contributed by industry—a growing source of private philanthropy—and by nonprofit foundations, or came from charitable bequests or income from investments of private welfare organizations. The list of private welfare groups is long and representative of all sorts of charities. Practically every community shares. United Givers Funds and Community Chests alone totaled 2,189 in 1962 and received over a half billion dollars for their aid to destitute children and families and for their work with the "Y's," Boy Scouts and Girl Scouts, settlement houses, hospital and nursing services, and similar participating organizations.

Then there are the church groups, the Red Cross, the various health organizations (providing research and help for the victims of everything from tuberculosis and heart disease to mental illness and muscular dystrophy), and a host of other organizations, most of whose good works are of significant public benefit. While their goals and activities have changed in recent years as government programs have expanded, they still play an important part in the nation's over-all welfare programs.

Fringe benefits Fastest growing of all welfare benefits have been the privately financed retirement, insurance, and other programs—the so-called "fringe benefits" of industry. They are the benefits whose financial value is over and above direct wage and salary payments. In addition to employer contributions to private retirement and welfare programs, they include paid vacations and holidays, paid sick leave, paid leave for military and jury duty, employers' required contributions to social security, supplemental unemployment benefits, severance or dismissal pay, profit-sharing plans, and annual bonuses.

As has been noted, retired workers covered by private pension plans in 1962 were receiving an average of $1,000 a year (exclusive of benefits under the social security program and other government retirement programs). In 1962, about 23 million individuals were covered by private pension plans.

Vacation pay has become increasingly liberal—the average worker in private industry now gets between two and three weeks of vacation plus an average of seven or eight paid holidays.

Paid sick leave is more common in offices than in industrial plants, but industrial workers generally are more apt to have sickness and accident insurance than are white-collar workers.

Most of the cost of these benefits is paid by employers—on their own initiative, or by law, or as the result of union contract provisions. But some benefits—pensions, for example—may be partly paid for through contributions by employees.

HOW FRINGE BENEFITS ADD TO THE HOURLY WAGE

vacation and other leave ●●●●● ●●●● ●●●

overtime, night, and other premium pay ●●●●● ●●●●

social insurance ●●●●● ●●●●

pensions and other private welfare plans ●●●●● ●●●●● ●●

Each symbol represents 1 cent per hour in fringe benefits paid by employers in 1959.

Cash value of the fringe benefits in rare instances can run as high as a dollar an hour over and above regular pay. In 1959, a government survey concluded that the value of employer-paid fringe benefits averaged 45 cents an hour—13 cents for paid leave, 10 cents for overtime pay, 10 cents for social security and other legally required payments, and 12 cents for private welfare plans. It is estimated that the value of major fringe benefits—excluding paid leave and premium pay —rose from less than 1 per cent of total wages and salaries in manufacturing in 1929 to over 10.5 per cent in 1962.

Total bill for welfare: $63 billion

In addition to the government-sponsored social insurance and public aid programs, there are also other government welfare services that, in a broad sense, are often included in "public welfare." These consist of health and medical programs and other welfare services for people receiving public aid under various programs, veterans' welfare programs, certain federal education services, and federal and state subsidies for low-cost housing. When all of these services are included, welfare expenditures, both public and private, totaled $63 billion in 1961. That was more than 12 per cent of the 1961 gross national product and it was two and a half times the 1950 bill.

This rapid rate of growth is expected to continue. As the government's social insurance programs embrace more types of workers, the costs and total outlays in benefits will go up. This will also be true of private pension plans and insurance programs. And as both public and private insurance programs are broadened, employee and employer contributions are likely to increase.

Tomorrow: billions more to finance welfare

There is also the likelihood that average benefits will increase, both because living costs will rise and because it will be considered desirable to raise benefits above levels adequate only for the most basic needs. So, again, there will be upward pressure on the costs of financing these benefits.

America's version of the "welfare state" is a combination of private and public programs whose costs are huge but whose benefits are considered indispensable. The pattern has been established in the past few decades. Future growth is expected to continue along the same lines.

CHAPTER XVI

Better Living in the Cities

FIRST CAME THE VILLAGES, then the towns, then the cities, then the sprawling metropolitan areas. Like inflating balloons, the small communities founded a century or two ago have grown larger and more complex. And as they have grown, problems that the founding fathers never foresaw have been generated—problems related to decent housing and pleasant surroundings and adequate transportation.

Seven out of ten live in urban areas Growth has been swift, with little attention to proper planning. In 1850, only 15 out of every 100 of the nation's 23 million people lived in a city or other urban area rather than on a farm. At the turn of the century, when population had reached 76 million, urban areas were home for 40 out of every 100 people. By 1950, 64 per cent of the country's 151 million residents lived in urban areas. And by 1960, the proportion was up to 70 per cent out of a total population of 179 million.

Also, by 1960, 62 per cent of all apartments and houses in the United States were in the 212 areas that the Census Bureau has designated as "standard metropolitan areas"—that is, areas that include one or more cities with a minimum of 50,000 population plus outlying suburbs. The 36.4 million houses and apartments in these areas represented a gain of about 9.3 million, or 34 per cent, in a decade. Inevitably, the increase has meant more congestion. Even worse are the serious deterioration and blight that accompany unplanned, hurried growth.

Slums . . . and what they breed One out of five of the houses in these areas is dilapidated or needs major repairs and alterations or lacks adequate plumbing facilities. Such houses are usually in crowded slums, often breeding grounds of poverty, delinquency, and crime. These substandard dwellings may be old tenements or houses that have seen better days. They may be shanties built years ago to accommodate industrial workers. They may be the jerry-built structures found in some factory towns. Not infrequently, a fairly new suburban community may have its share of deterioration because of poorly planned or inferior housing developments. About three fifths of the dilapidated areas are outside large metropolitan centers, mostly in small cities and communities.

PEOPLE MOVE TO THE CITIES AND SUBURBS

It is estimated that by 1980, 72 out of 100 people will be living in Standard Metropolitan Areas.

living **outside** Standard Metropolitan Areas | living **in** Standard Metropolitan Areas

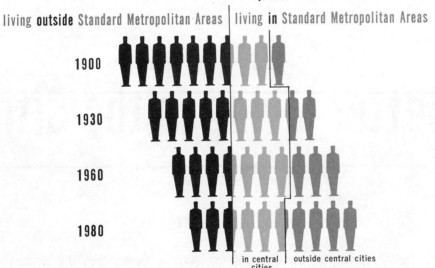

1900
1930
1960
1980

in central cities | outside central cities

Each symbol represents 10 per cent of total U.S. population.

Some flee, others cannot Those who can manage to do so flee these areas. They seek better sections of the city. Or, more likely, they move to the suburbs in their search for a better way of life. Usually, it is those with low incomes or the victims of racial discrimination who remain in the slums, either by choice or necessity.

INCREASED HOUSING, 1950-1960

Most of the new housing of recent years has been built in the suburbs.

outside Standard Metropolitan Areas

in Standard Metropolitan Areas

in central cities

outside central cities

Each symbol represents an increase of 1 million housing units.

Blighted and dilapidated areas constitute a cancer within the city. They produce tragic human suffering. Once formed, they spread and grow, degrading everything they touch. Most of the nation's cities bear the scars of this deterioration. Central metropolitan areas, particularly, exhibit the destructive effects of unchecked blight.

Everyone suffers: businessmen whose trade is hurt; cultural institutions left as islands in seas of dilapidation; transport systems choked by narrow streets; city governments deprived of millions in taxation as property loses its value.

Solution: replace the slums

The way to stop the blight is to remove it and replace it with modern, attractive areas according to a large-scale plan. Achieving this goal has been a joint effort of federal, state, and local governments and of private industry. Hundreds of urban renewal and redevelopment projects are the fruit of this cooperation. Replacement of slums with new housing, office buildings, industrial structures, cultural and educational centers, parks, playgrounds, and roads is the basic goal.

Usually, the federal government provides funds for surveys and lends money to local authorities to buy and clear the land in slum areas, preparatory to rebuilding, and to relocate slum dwellers in new homes.

Local governments clear the land, erect public buildings, such as schools and libraries, and sell or lease sites to private builders to construct new houses, shopping centers, etc., following the master plan. Leasing or selling of the cleared land is usually at a loss; the federal government absorbs part of the loss through subsidies to redevelopment authorities.

As of April 30, 1963, the federal government, through the Urban Renewal Administration, had spent or allocated $3.2 billion over a period of 14 years as its share of the nation's massive redevelopment undertakings. About 1,400 urban renewal projects located in 691 communities were involved.

DECLINE OF THE CENTRAL CITIES

Major central cities within Standard Metropolitan Areas which lost population, 1950-1960.

CONDITION OF METROPOLITAN HOUSING

Nearly 14 per cent of the nation's homes in 1960 were either deteriorated or in a dilapidated state.

SOUND
—with all plumbing facilities

SOUND
—but lacking some plumbing

DETERIORATING

DILAPIDATED

Each symbol represents 10 per cent of all housing units in Standard Metropolitan Statistical Areas, 1960.

A major worry has always been what happens to the thousands of slum families who lose their homes as a result of redevelopment. Unless public housing is included in a project, few can afford to return to their former neighborhoods. Under the law, homes must be found for them before redevelopment can proceed. Of 150,000 families displaced by urban renewal by the end of 1962, all but about 10,000, or 7 per cent, were able to find better housing than had previously been their lot.

Many small businessmen have also been displaced, as bulldozers swept away their shops and stores. They, too, represent a serious problem for redevelopment officials. Sometimes—but by no means always—they are able to resume business in the redeveloped area.

Results of a $3.2 billion effort

Around the country, impressive results are to be seen from this attack on the slums. Pittsburgh's "Golden Triangle," Philadelphia's Society Hill development, Washington's Southwest development project, St. Louis' massive downtown rehabilitation, and New Haven's revival of a dilapidated central area are examples of what has been accomplished. Many others could be cited.

A by-product of urban redevelopment has been a series of additions to the nation's cultural wealth—New York's Lincoln Center for the Performing Arts; Washington's Arena Stage; Asheville's Civic Arts Center; a stadium, symphony hall, art and industrial museum, and theater in Pittsburgh; a civic auditorium in Grand Rapids; libraries in Norfolk, Jersey City, Minneapolis, Port Huron, and Fargo. All are parts of redevelopment areas, once sites of ugly slums.

Another by-product has been new revenues in city taxes from areas that once produced very little. Detroit, Oakland, and Pittsburgh are among cities reporting this welcome benefit.

Redevelopment trends

New trends in redevelopment are taking shape in the 1960s. For example:

● There is renewed emphasis on rehabilitating existing structures rather than tearing them down. Rehabilitation is cheaper, and it enables the residents to keep their homes and merchants to keep their businesses.

● Long-range programs for local improvement are being established.

By the end of 1962, 1,836 communities had such programs.

● Federal, state, and local funds are being used to create long-term development plans for sprawling areas with common problems of transportation, utilities, services, and so on. Hopefully, this will prevent a recurrence of the difficulties that grew from lack of planning in the past.

● Through a similar cooperative effort, again with the help of federal money, state and local agencies are setting aside open land for recreation, conservation, and future development before the space is gobbled up by urban sprawl. By April 30, 1963, 13 projects had been started. Such land cannot be used for building purposes.

PROGRESS IN URBAN RENEWAL

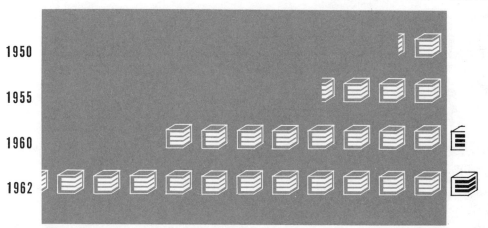

Each symbol represents 100 projects.

Lifting the face of American cities is a tremendously costly and complex undertaking. By early 1963, many billions of dollars had been spent or allocated, by both public and private sources, to get the job done.

In 1962 alone, the division of costs for a total of 492 urban renewal projects was as follows:

	amount (millions)	per cent
Total	$ 5,813	100.0
Private housing	2,100	36.1
Public housing	83	1.4
Commercial	1,286	22.1
Industrial	538	9.3
Public and semipublic (including site improvements and facilities)	1,806	31.1

Can the nation catch up? Many experts say that even these huge amounts are just a drop in the bucket. New York City, for example, with an area of 320 square miles, has undertaken only 3 square miles of redevelopment. Some authorities doubt that the nation can ever catch up with its urban deterioration. And they are concerned with the spread of urban sprawl in the densely populated areas on the East Coast, in the Midwest, and on the West Coast—all areas where major cities grow toward each other until their metropolitan areas ultimately overlap. With vast amounts of open space being lost by helter-skelter growth, such areas will inevitably produce great segments of blight.

Measure of success Nevertheless, the record is encouraging. In 10 years, from 1950 to 1960, the number of dilapidated houses and apartments dropped from 5 million to 3.6 million. Urban renewal programs can take part of the credit for this. In some communities—Washington and Philadelphia, for example—rehabilitation of downtown areas has been so successful that many families who had fled the blight have now returned to the city.

The United States today is predominantly a nation of city dwellers. Only by persistent and unceasing effort and expenditure of money is the country likely to keep abreast of its cities' needs in the years to come.

CHAPTER XVII

Forest, Field, and Stream

NO MATTER HOW INDUSTRIALIZED A SOCIETY BECOMES, it cannot exist without the bounty of its soil. Its croplands produce food and fiber to feed and clothe the people. Its grazing areas sustain dairy herds, sheep, goats, beef cattle, and other livestock. Its springs and ponds and streams and rivers and lakes are sources of indispensable water for agriculture, industry, and home.

The American land

The United States is particularly blessed with natural resources. The area of the 48 contiguous states is 1.9 billion acres. Hawaii and Alaska add another 369 million acres. Nine out of ten of these acres supply farm products, lumber, or minerals. The rest is barren or has been converted to sites for cities, industrial developments, parks, highways, and other attributes of a modern civilization.

From the days of the earliest settlers, America found its greatness in the land. The lush forests, the fertile fields, the rich mineral resources, the swiftly running streams and rivers provided the young nation with all that it needed to grow and prosper.

Without these resources, there could have been no thriving cities. Industry could not have developed as it did. There would not have been the bountiful farms and the lumber mills and the great hydroelectric power dams that dot the land.

But in their haste to grow, the people did not always recognize that their natural wealth was not inexhaustible. They did not take measures to preserve what they had. And they often misused the land's resources.

101

CROPLAND

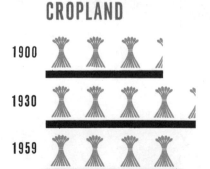

1900

1930

1959

Each symbol represents 100 million acres.

The decline in cropland since 1930 partly reflects more scientific cultivation methods, which increased the crop yield per acre and decreased the need for acreage under cultivation.

GRASSLAND

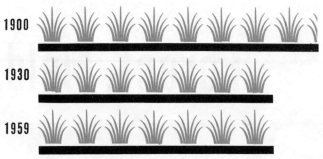

1900

1930

1959

Each symbol represents 100 million acres.

In the first three decades of this century, acreage in grassland in the United States decreased. In part, this decrease was due to neglect of the land until the 1930s, when stringent conservation measures were instituted.

FOREST AND WOODLAND

1900

1930

1959

Each symbol represents 100 million acres.

Penalty of neglect Over the years, a third of the nation's forest lands have been converted to cropland or denuded by fire and flood. About 200 million acres, or one fifth of the grasslands and green prairies that once covered almost half the country, have been lost to other uses. Millions of acres of cropland are so eroded and overworked as to be useless.

The problem is not unique to the United States. In Western Europe, too, there was a long history of neglect of the land and of failure to replace what was removed or to restore what had been overworked. But there, a concentrated effort has been underway since the nineteenth century to remedy the mistakes of the past through modern conservation methods.

How the nation acted to conserve its riches

Until the 1930s, U.S. attempts to conserve land resources were of only modest proportions. Then came a massive effort to repair the accumulated damage of many generations. A government program was launched to end flagrant misuse of the land—such practices as overgrazing, unscientific farming methods, indifference to the damage of wind and water erosion. Farmers were encouraged to plant cover crops. They were urged to adopt scientific cultivation techniques: contour farming, strip-cropping, mulching, terracing. They received help in building farm ponds to control moisture and drainage systems to stem erosion.

Here is the score for these and other conservation achievements between 1936 and 1960:

Terraces placed on 25.4 million acres.
Field and contour strip-cropping on 110.6 million acres.
Permanent vegetative cover added to 339.6 million acres.
Trees and shrubs planted on 3 million acres.
Drainage of 40.1 million acres.
Deferred grazing (to permit natural seeding) on 218.2 million acres.

In addition, by the early 1960s, farmers were using three times as much fertilizer as they had used in 1940, to compensate for exhausted soil nutrients. And the quality of the fertilizer was much better than in the past. Its nitrogen content was nearly triple what it had been. The use of another vital ingredient, potash, had doubled. Growers now return as much nitrogen and phosphates to the soil as are consumed by their crops, though not quite as much potash.

Damage continues

It is an impressive record, but it is not enough. About a quarter of the country's cropland is still being critically damaged by erosion. Another quarter is subject to less serious erosion. Grazing lands have suffered tremendously over the years, and it is estimated that about half the government-owned rangelands west of the Mississippi are in bad condition.

What the forests provide

Like the crop and grazing lands, the country's forests are indispensable to many of its basic needs. They provide billions of feet of timber a year for everything from houses to packing boxes. They produce raw materials for the expanding chemical, textile, paper, and plastic industries. The forests are nature's refuge for animals and birds, and they are man's retreat for camping, hiking, hunting, and fishing. Most of all, they hold the soil on slopes and hills, prevent floods from sweeping down river valleys, and retain moisture in the land.

Of the approximately 610 million acres of forest and woodlands in the 48 contiguous states, about 163 million are on privately owned farmlands; the rest is outside of farms. Roughly four out of five acres are suitable for growing timber of commercial quality. The rest is scrub growth or otherwise not useful for lumbering.

National forests make up about a fourth of the total forest land in the continental United States. If the national forests were combined into one single forest, they would cover an area equal to New England, New York, Pennsylvania, and the Atlantic coastline states as far south as North Carolina.

103

It takes some 25 years for many types of trees to grow big enough to be commercially useful. Obviously, long-term planning is needed to maintain the forest reserves at present levels or to increase them. One estimate is that unless more trees are cultivated and forests replenished with new growth, in the not too distant future the country will be able to produce only two thirds of its lumber requirements.

Forests must be cut according to modern methods if natural reforestation is to occur. That means selective cutting, cleaning out of timber with no economic value, and replanting of areas where nature fails to sustain a proper rate of growth to meet commercial needs.

In recent years, less than half the forest areas were being managed in such a way as to provide for future needs.

LAND DRAINED AND IRRIGATED

Through these methods of land management, millions of acres have been successfully restored to cultivation.

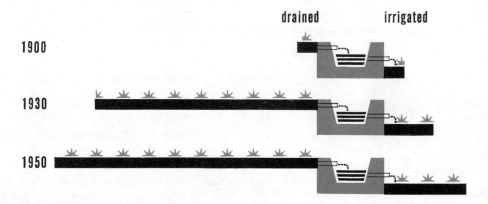

Each symbol represents 10 million acres.

Control of forest fires Control of forest fires has for years been a major concern of the nation, and millions of acres are now protected against devastating fire by such measures as firebreaks through thick forests, erection of forest towers at strategic points, and employment of airplanes, radio communications, and other modern devices for rapid detection of fires. Education against carelessness by campers, hikers, hunters, and picnickers is a prime weapon; 7 out of 10 forest fires are caused by human carelessness. Lightning causes some of the most serious forest fires.

In 1940, 26 million acres of forests were burned out; in 1950, 15.5 million acres; in 1962, only 4 million acres. The $64 million spent on fire detection and control in 1962 undoubtedly helped hold down the damage inflicted by the 105,000 forest fires that year.

With population growing, industrial activity rising, and irrigation requirements intensifying, water is a priority item in planning for tomorrow. For every gallon consumed each day in 1900, eight gallons were needed in 1960. The national daily requirements are expected to be close to a half trillion gallons by 1980—compared with 1960's 323 billion gallons.

The 323 billion gallons used daily in 1960 consisted only in small part of the water that came out of household faucets—about 22 billion gallons. Water's biggest consumers were industry and utilities (160 billion gallons a day) and irrigation (135 billion gallons a day to irrigate about 33 million acres of land).

The nation depends on its rivers and lakes not only for the water consumed in industry, farm, and home, but also for movement of barges, cargo vessels, and other water transport, and for fishing, swimming, and other recreational purposes.

Flood control

Conserving this precious resource involves several different and gigantic undertakings. Flood control has long been a basic goal of national planning, and by 1962 nearly 6 million acres had been set aside by the federal government for flood control.

Cleaning up the major rivers and waterways to rid them of pollution is another goal, one that will require many years to achieve. An estimated 50 per cent of the nation's communities empty their wastes and raw sewage into rivers and streams without benefit of sewage treatment plants. In addition, innumerable industrial plants contaminate water supplies. Only when this pollution is cleaned up can these water resources be reclaimed for recreational and other uses.

Fresh water from salt water

One of the most hopeful developments toward creating additional water supplies has been the effort to convert salt water to fresh water through desalinization processes. A number of different methods, including atomic techniques, are being experimented with, though so far all are costly.

Finally, many of the 160 major river basins in the nation are potential sites of combined flood control, water conservation, and hydroelectric developments. Among them are the Columbia, Ohio, Missouri, and Colorado river basins.

If the total flow of all U.S. river basins could be distributed where it is needed most, there would be no water problem. The nation would have more than its needs. Unfortunately, this cannot be done. Thus, in some regions the situation is worse than in others.

In the East and also in Missouri, Arkansas, Iowa, and portions of Minnesota, Kansas, Oklahoma, and Louisiana, rainfall and water supply are normally plentiful. Adequate storage facilities for water and pollution control are the basic needs here.

In the Great Plains, Texas, the Rocky Mountain area, California, and part of Oregon, the problem is water shortage. The region has only one fifth the water supply of the East, but it uses four times as much. So acute is the problem that the Supreme Court has had to render a decision allocating the use of Colorado River waters between Arizona and California. Mexican users in Sonora and Baja California have also claimed water rights here, further complicating the issue.

The Pacific Northwest (Washington, Idaho, most of Oregon, and part of Montana) is partly humid and partly arid but has a sufficiently large stream flow to meet its needs. Its major challenge is to develop the vast hydroelectric potential of the Columbia River.

Investment for tomorrow

Billions of dollars will have to be spent in the years ahead to maintain and restore America's croplands, forests, and water resources, Land will be reclaimed through drainage and irrigation projects. Millions of acres of forests will be made more productive through replanting and extension of forest preservation methods. Increasing water supplies will inevitably be related to the success of antipollution measures and planning of river valley developments.

The total costs will be huge. But the dividends will be priceless in meeting the needs of tomorrow's Americans.

CHAPTER XVIII

Changing Resources

AMERICANS HAVE BEEN BROUGHT UP in a tradition of almost inexhaustible plenty, and they are not likely to think of their country as a "have-not" nation. Their mines have had rich lodes of ores and minerals. Their oil and gas wells have spouted forth abundant quantities of energy-producing fuel. Rarely has the United States experienced a serious lack of raw materials to build and expand with.

Historic switch But now the nation is well into an era when it can no longer boast of being almost self-sufficient in its resources. Industry's ravenous appetite for raw materials has become more and more demanding, while the supply has been decreasing. The situation is not as serious as feared only a few years ago, but the United States now is definitely labeled a have-not country for many vital materials, a label it will have to live with in the years ahead.

This development comes as no surprise. For decades, the nation's industry has consumed as much of some raw materials as the rest of the world combined. With only 6 per cent of the world's population, the United States has in the past used enough ore to account for half the world's steel output, and has consumed more than half the world's oil and about nine tenths of its natural gas.

America's prodigal past Being well endowed with most of its raw material needs, the country could easily afford to use materials in these huge amounts. Year after year, the United States was the leading producer of iron ore, copper, aluminum, lead, zinc, coal, petroleum, natural gas, sulphur, phosphates, cement, and gypsum—as well as of such metals as molybdenum and vanadium, used to produce steel alloys. But beginning in 1940 the need for raw materials began to exceed the domestic supplies.

Behind this transition was a rapid and unprecedented surge in industrial activity. From 1940 to 1961, the nation's consumption of all minerals about doubled. Despite growing efficiency in industry and an exhaustive search for new sources, the gap between what the country produces in raw materials and what it consumes has widened significantly.

The relatively few raw materials still being produced in amounts exceeding domestic needs include coal, molybdenum, cement, natural gas, sulphur, phosphate rock, and magnesium. For other basic raw materials —petroleum, bauxite, lead, copper, iron ore, potash, and zinc—the nation has turned increasingly to sources outside its borders. These must be added to the list of vital raw materials that the United States has always imported—tin, chromite, manganese, nickel, and rubber.

GROWTH IN RAW MATERIALS CONSUMPTION

In the first 40 years of the century, U. S. consumption of raw materials more than doubled. It increased by 38 per cent in the next 20 years.

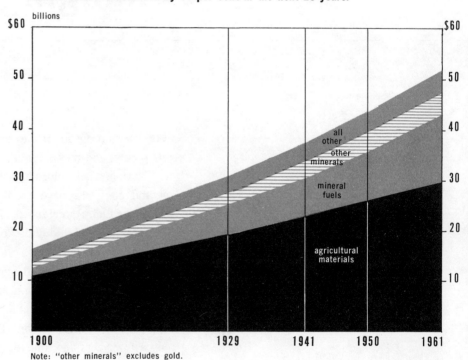

Note: "other minerals" excludes gold.

Growing need to import For other resources, too, there has been a growing need to turn elsewhere for supplies. The country's fisheries are unable to meet the demand for varied seafood products. The need to import furs is of long standing. Many forest products—particularly pulpwood—are also imported.

How does a nation cope with such a shift in the adequacy of its natural resources? A number of things can be done and are being done to adapt to the change.

Conservation of resources Conservation, of course, is a major weapon. Conservation of land, water supply, and forests (as described in the preceding chapter) is basic to any long-term program for protection of natural resources. With proper measures, such resources can actually be renewed and expanded.

SELF-SUFFICIENCY IN SELECTED MINERALS, 1961

Except for bituminous coal, industry is dependent on sources abroad for most of its basic materials, including oil, copper, nickel, and industrial diamonds.

Each mineral symbol represents 10 per cent of U. S. consumption. Black boats represent imports; white boats, exports or surplus.

In addition, ingenious methods have been developed for tapping new domestic sources of needed raw materials, such as extracting magnesium from the sea.

Impressive as such developments are, they do not solve the problem of maintaining supplies of all the basic raw materials indispensable to the American economy. The United States is constantly looking for additional reserves of the materials it needs and developing new methods of using what it has.

Tapping new sources Some of the new sources are right at home. For example:

● When the high-quality iron ores in the Lake Superior region began to run out, methods were developed for utilizing the lower grade taconite ores found in the same area.

● At one time, coal was strip-mined only if it was actually on or close to the surface, but now the process of strip-mining is used even if 100 feet of cover must be removed to reach the vein.

● Oil wells have been drilled progressively deeper; today the drills go down nearly five miles in the search for the "black gold."

PRODUCTIVITY IN BITUMINOUS COAL MINING

For each man-hour of labor in 1961 nearly two and a half times as much bituminous coal was produced as in 1947, and more than three times as much as in 1935.

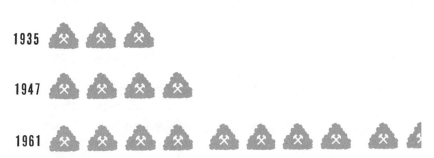

Each symbol represents 25 per cent of 1947 output per man-hour.

- Methods have been developed for refining low-grade copper ores which in the past would not have been mined for lack of proper refining facilities.

Exit the pick-and-shovel prospector

Closely related to this approach is the use of new scientific methods for uncovering reserves. Airborne magnetometers are used to map natural gas, oil, and other mineral deposits. Geochemistry—the chemical analysis of soils, rocks, water, etc.—is employed to uncover mineral concentrations. The pick-and-shovel prospector is almost extinct.

Developing sources of supply abroad has solved some of industry's needs for raw materials. New and rich iron-ore deposits in Labrador and Venezuela, and oil fields in the Middle East and other parts of the globe supplement the inadequate supplies at home.

Sometimes the reverse happens. When the country's tungsten supply in Communist China was cut off, domestic exploration was pushed and in a few years the shortage was overcome.

PRIMARY ENERGY PRODUCTION

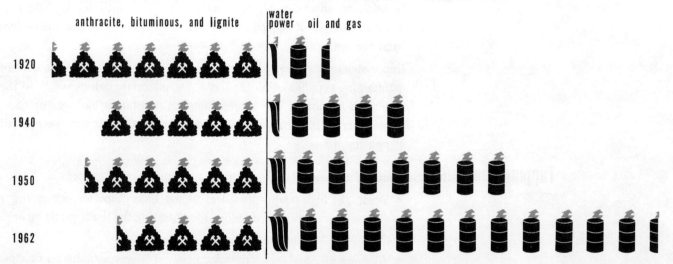

Each symbol represents 100 million tons of coal equivalent.

Stretching raw materials

Making raw materials stretch further is another way of meeting the problem. Manufacturers of tin plate make their tin ingots go 60 per cent further by using electroplating instead of the hot-dip method of manufacture. Diesel locomotives, which have practically replaced the iron horses of yore, are seven times as efficient in the use of fuel as steam locomotives and twice as efficient as electrified locomotives.

A more recent trend is miniaturization and more efficient design. Transistor radios, compact cars, smaller motors, streamlined machinery and equipment, and lightweight but strong metals all reflect this trend. One pipeline company saved 36,000 tons of steel by specifying a thinner but stronger steel casing than usual for a 400-mile gas pipeline.

The art of improving on nature

Substitution plays an important part in the effort to make materials go further. Everyone is aware of the extensive use of plastics to replace metals and wood. Modern plastics are strong, durable, and resistant to heat and cold. The rapid rise in the use of synthetic fibers for clothing has lessened the nation's dependency on imported wool. Synthetic rubber is now available in such quantities as to make the nation no longer vulnerable to a sudden cutoff of natural rubber supplies from abroad. All sorts of by-products of oil are emerging from the chemist's test tubes to replace natural materials. Coal tar is another chemical source of everything from dyes to wonder drugs.

The most impressive development of recent years has been the splitting of the atom to produce electrical energy. In time, it is expected that power plants will no longer be dependent on traditional fuels to drive their generators, but extensive use of nuclear power is not likely for many years. In the meantime, the nation has substantial untapped reserves of hydropower to conserve dwindling supplies of coal and oil used for power generation. As of January 1, 1962, undeveloped water power was estimated to equal about 113 million kilowatts of installed capacity.

Installed generating capacity of hydroelectric plants increased from 2.8 million kilowatts to 38 million kilowatts in the half century between 1912 and 1962. But as a per cent of total installed power capacity in the country, it fell from 25 to 18. Thus, by 1962, the nation was getting a smaller proportion of its power from hydroelectric sources than it had a half century earlier. As a matter of fact, 82 per cent of its total electric power in 1962 came from plants fueled with coal, oil, gas, wood and, to a very minor degree, nuclear fuel.

Meeting future demand for electric energy will involve more extensive development of hydropower as well as advances in the use of atomic power.

ELECTRIC POWER FOR AN EXPANDING ECONOMY

Between 1950 and 1962, the nation's power generators had to boost their output more than 100 per cent to keep up with industrial and consumer demand.

1922

1940

1950

1962

Each symbol represents 50 billion KWH.

Titanium, germanium, silicon No one knows what materials now considered surplus for industrial purposes will suddenly come into demand. Titanium, long an element of only scientific curiosity, became irreplaceable in the development of the rocket program. Germanium, of absolutely no utility a few years ago, is the raw material of transistors, used in place of vacuum tubes in radios, TV sets, and electronic equipment. The second most abundant element, silicon, is the principal ingredient of glass. In recent years, it has been used to make glass fibers that can be spun or woven into all sorts of shapes, and to produce silicones, indispensable in the manufacture of synthetic rubber, plastics, and protective coatings.

111

Progress brings industrial changes and these in turn alter the kinds of raw materials that the country consumes. Thus, aluminum and magnesium are of growing importance to the economy; coal doesn't occupy quite the dominant position it used to. Organic chemicals, light metals, liquid fuel, and natural gas are other examples of the stuff of modern manufacturing.

Assignment for tomorrow

Like Western Europe, the United States will have to look elsewhere for many of its raw materials, particularly to the undeveloped areas of Africa, Asia, and South America. Its dependency on imports from every corner of the globe will mount. It will also have to conserve carefully its remaining natural resources. It will have to intensify its efforts to extract more of what it has at home, to substitute new materials for depleted or nearly depleted resources, and to discover new ways of using materials that in the past have been considered of little practical value.

CHAPTER XIX

Farms, Farmers, and Food

THE ENDLESS AGRICULTURAL CYCLE of sowing, tilling, and reaping, is as old as civilization itself, but nowhere has it come to such bountiful fulfillment as in the United States. America's farms are a priceless resource, their harvests adequate not only to the country's needs but to the needs of millions of people in other lands.

Agriculture: underpinning of the economy

Unlike most countries, the United States has no worries about the ability of its farmers to meet the food and fiber needs of the nation. On the contrary, its major agricultural challenge is managing its food surpluses.

The accomplishments of the nation's farmers have been astounding. For over 25 years, output has been rising sharply, with only slight pauses in the upward trend. Between 1950 and 1962, there was a 25 per cent jump—to a market value of $39 billion—in the production of crops, livestock, and livestock products.

At the source of this bounty are not quite 300 million acres of land on which crops are grown. In addition, there is a slowly increasing population of dairy cows, beef cattle, poultry, and other livestock. Between 1950 and 1962, the number of livestock increased by about 13 per cent.

Who benefits?

There are two beneficiaries of this agricultural wealth:

● The American people eat well. In 1962, they consumed about 1,455 pounds of food per person, including 165 pounds of beef, veal, lamb, and pork. This is higher than the meat consumption in any other country except cattle-rich Argentina, Australia, New Zealand, and Uruguay.

• The United States is a prime source of food for other nations of the world. One quarter of U. S. exports consists of food. The value of these exports in 1962 was $5 billion, an increase of $1.7 billion over average annual exports in the early 1950s. Of total U. S. food production, the proportion shipped overseas rose from 9 per cent in 1950 to 14 per cent in 1962.

AGRICULTURAL EXPORTS, 1962

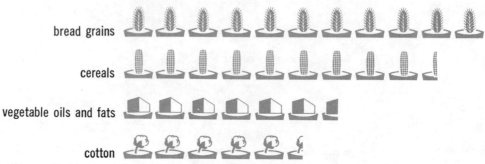

bread grains

cereals

vegetable oils and fats

cotton

tobacco

all other

Each symbol represents $100 million worth of agricultural products exported.

What the United States sells More than two fifths of the value of United States agricultural exports consists of bread grains and other cereals. The United States also exports hundreds of millions of dollars' worth of fats and oils and supplies much of the world's cotton and tobacco. In 1962, for example, it exported over half a billion dollars' worth of cotton and about a third of a billion dollars' worth of tobacco—33 per cent of the world exports of cotton, and 29 per cent of total world tobacco exports.

What it buys Though the United States is a big exporter of farm products, it also imports around $4 billion worth of agricultural products every year. The imports include large amounts of products that can't be grown domestically—such as bananas, cocoa, coffee, tea, and spices. In addition, the country bought $600 million worth of meat products in 1962, primarily fresh or frozen boneless beef, canned hams, and canned beef.

Secret of American farm productivity How do American farmers do it? How have they produced surpluses year after year, while many parts of the world have great difficulty maintaining harvests sufficient to meet mounting demands?

The answer lies in part in good climate over much of the food-growing area of the country and in part in the years of broadening conservation practices and increasing use of irrigation. But, most important, it lies in the application of scientific techniques in the cultivation and harvesting of major crops.

Machinery does the work Mechanization of U. S. farms has proceeded at a fantastic pace ever since World War I. And there has been no letup in recent years. American farmers boasted three times as many tractors in 1962 as in 1940,

114

nearly three times as many trucks, five times as many grain combines, nearly nine times as many corn pickers, more than three times as many pickup balers, and four times as many field forage harvesters.

AGRICULTURAL IMPORTS, 1962

coffee, tea, and spices	
meat and edible animal products	
sugar and related products	
vegetables, fruits, and nuts	
crude rubber	
wool	
all other	

Each symbol represents $100 million worth of agricultural products imported.

The horse, of course, has been irrevocably displaced by the tractor as the farmer's main source of muscle power. In 1962, with about 4.7 million tractors in use, farmers had almost two of these mechanized work-savers for each horse or mule. As recently as 1950, the reverse was true—there were more than two horses and mules on the farm for each tractor.

Machines not only displace animals. They increase tremendously what each farm worker can accomplish in a day's labor.

The result has been a constantly diminishing number of laborers on farms and an expanding work load handled by those who remain.

ewer farm workers—higher output per man

Between 1950 and 1962, the number of workers on American farms declined from 7.5 million to 5.2 million, while the number of acres cultivated per worker rose from about 45 to over 55. Productivity of farmers has been moving upward for over 20 years. The amount of production for each man-hour of labor almost doubled between 1940 and 1950, and it almost doubled again in the next 12 years.

The yield per acre of many basic crops has also been constantly expanding. A big reason has been tremendous advances in the effectiveness of fertilizers, pesticides, and insecticides. Agricultural chemists have performed minor miracles in recent years in backing up nature.

Another reason for better yields has been vastly improved seed stocks. Hybrid corn seeds, for example, have helped raise the corn harvest from an average of 27 bushels per acre prior to 1940 to more than 50 bushels today. Output per acre in cotton doubled between the 1920s and the 1950s.

Equally impressive have been the achievements in better livestock breeding methods. Farmers get more beef per pound of feed today than they ever got in the past. They are able to grow chickens and turkeys and hogs much faster and with larger proportions of edible meat. Hens lay more eggs, cows give more milk.

FEWER FARMERS AND ACRES, MORE PRODUCTION

Though farm population dropped between 1950 and 1962, and the number of harvested acres also declined, crop and livestock production increased, thanks to better cultivation techniques.

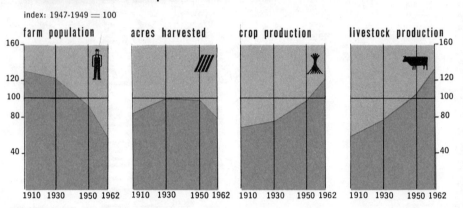

index: 1947-1949 = 100

Problems among plenty   Such phenomenal achievements are not without their problems.

For example, there is general agreement that, if desired, the country's farms could push their production far beyond current levels, simply by plowing more land and intensifying cultivation of existing acres. Actually, it has been national policy for many years to discourage such efforts and to try to curtail the piling up of surpluses of farm products.

Crop control and price supports   The federal government spends about $5 billion annually to restrain overplanting, to assure farmers of a good return on their crops, and to encourage conservation practices. Of that $5 billion (6 per cent of the total federal budget), about $3.4 billion goes to support minimum prices, pay for crop control measures, and subsidize soil conservation measures. Most of the rest is used to help farmers sell their products abroad.

While they are interrelated, the government's price support program and its crop control program have contradictory results. The price supports stimulate production of agricultural surpluses; farmers strive to produce as much as they can on the land available for cultivation. The crop controls, on the other hand, are designed to limit harvests. Farmers are paid to limit the number of acres used for crops. At the core of much of the discussion over the nation's agricultural policies has been the dilemma created by the inconsistencies of these two programs.

Another problem is related to the changing rural economy.

Less and less is this a country of small farms dependent mostly on the labor of the farmer and his family. Edward Higbee, in his Twentieth Century Fund report, *Farms and Farmers in an Urban Age,* figures that even a modest farm requires $42,000 worth of equipment and supplies—an investment well beyond the resources of the typical small farmer.

Decline of the small farm   Many small farms have, therefore, been abandoned or have been merged with other farms. Between 1940 and 1962, the number of farms in the nation dropped from 6.4 million to about 3.7 million. In 1940, the average farm consisted of 174 acres; in 1962, the average was 315 acres.

The figures below show the shift from small to large farms over the last two decades:

size of farm (acres)	per cent of all farms		
	1940	1950	1959
total	100.0	100.0	100.0
under 10	8.3	9.0	6.5
10–49	29.2	27.5	21.9
50–99	21.2	19.5	17.8
100–179	21.5	20.5	20.8
180–259	8.0	9.0	11.2
260–499	7.5	8.9	12.7
500–999	2.7	3.4	5.4
1,000 and over	1.6	2.2	3.7

Bigness is taking over

Bigness is becoming as characteristic of farms as of business, labor, and government. By the early 1960s, over half the nation's farmland was in the 4 per cent of the farms that had 1,000 acres or more. (Not all of this farmland was used for crops; much of it was idle or being used for pasture or woodland.) These farms harvested about a fifth of all the cropland. If the farms of 500 acres and over are included, big farms accounted for about 40 per cent of the country's harvested cropland. Yet in number, they represented only 9 per cent of all U. S. farms.

ONE FARM WORKER FEEDS OVER 28 PEOPLE

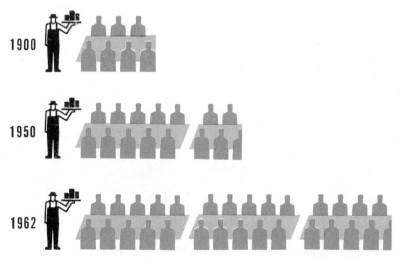

1900

1950

1962

Each colored symbol represents one person supplied with food and fibers.

In 1959, the total value of farm products originating on farms with annual sales of $10,000 or more came to $21.9 billion. This was three fourths of the value of all farm products sold in the country that year. But the farms on which these crops were grown made up only two fifths of all the nation's farms. They averaged about 800 acres each, and comprised two thirds of the nation's farm lands.

Exodus to the city

It is not surprising that millions of people have left the farms because they could no longer make a living. Between 1940 and 1962, farm

117

population dropped more than 50 per cent. More than 23 million people left the farms as family heads switched from agriculture to other occupations. One out of four people lived on farms in 1940; today the figure is less than one out of twelve. Never again will the United States call itself a nation of farmers.

Problems for tomorrow

Progress has its penalties, and seldom has this truth been so amply demonstrated as in the historic transition that has changed U. S. farm life in little more than a generation. The future of American farming will be a continuation of the present picture: bigness, growing productivity, declining dependence on traditional farm labor. No one doubts that agriculture will be able to meet the demands placed on it—domestic or foreign. But the problems that grow out of this bountiful resource will persist in plaguing the nation.

CHAPTER XX

A Nation Among Nations

NO COUNTRY STANDS ALONE—isolated and self-sufficient and able to prosper without benefit of trade with other nations. Trade is the cement that binds nations together in an ever-shrinking world. It produces interchange of ideas as well as of goods, and it can help increase mutual understanding and respect.

Trade: binder of nations

The importance of trade in the life of the average U. S. citizen is easy to see. His cup of coffee in the morning, the wool in his clothing and rugs, the copper in his home, and the tin in the containers of his canned fruits and vegetables are but random examples of what trade with other nations brings. Without such trade, Americans could not have many of the conveniences that they are accustomed to.

Likewise, from trade come jobs for the millions of Americans who produce the goods that industry sells abroad. Whether it is the auto worker in Detroit or the wheat grower in North Dakota, foreign markets for the products of their labor are vital to their jobs and businesses.

Balance sheet for U.S. trade

The United States occupies a major position in world trade in both the extent and the nature of its dealing with other nations. Since 1950, goods shipped out of the country have amounted to between 17 and 21 per cent of the world's total exports. Goods brought into the country have accounted for between 13 and 16 per cent of the world's imports.

The dollar amounts involved are substantial, even though they represent only a small proportion of the goods and services produced and consumed annually in the United States. At the beginning of the 1960s, exports were running over $20 billion a year—about 7 per cent of the nation's total output of movable goods.

Imports averaged between $15 billion and $17 billion a year at the start of the decade, or about 6 per cent of domestic goods output.

Foreign trade is not as vital to the U. S. economy as to the economies of most other industrial nations, but it nevertheless plays an important part in sustaining the country's economic tempo.

U. S. FOREIGN TRADE, 1921-1962

As foreign trade has grown, the U. S. export surplus has increased.

Each symbol represents $2 billion worth of foreign trade.

Customers overseas seek two major types of goods from this country. First, they buy manufactured products—the products of industry and factories. Since 1950, exports of manufactured goods have amounted to about 75 to 80 per cent of total exports. Increasingly, the United States has been a major world source for products ready to be used in their manufactured state.

What the United States sells abroad The list of such products includes almost everything made in the United States. But far and away the most important export products are machinery to equip foreign factories, and automobiles and trucks to provide transport. Together these accounted for well over $8 billion in exports in 1962. In addition, exports of chemicals came to almost $2 billion and exports of metals and metal goods, exclusive of machinery, to over $1.6 billion.

Aside from manufactured goods, the nation's major exports consist of agricultural products: corn, wheat, other cereal grains, cotton, vegetable oils, tobacco, and other farm crops. In 1962, they accounted for about a quarter of all exports, a proportion that hasn't changed much since 1950. Foreign customers are vitally important to U. S. farmers. About one out of five acres of farmland harvested is devoted to products for sale abroad. In the 1960s, the quantity of farm products sent abroad was about 8 times as high as that of 20 years earlier.

Obviously, any reduction of markets abroad for American agricultural output is of very serious concern at home, particularly when viewed against the problem of crop surpluses.

What foreign nations sell to this country

From overseas, Americans buy all manner of goods—transistor radios, typewriters, cameras, sewing machines, clothing, clocks and watches, and other consumer products. But while these may be easy to spot, they are not the nation's major imports. In 1962 these were oil and oil products ($1.8 billion); machinery, trucks, and automobiles ($1.7 billion); iron, steel, and ferroalloys ($1.5 billion); nonferrous metals, such as copper and tin ($1.2 billion); newsprint and paper products ($1.2 billion); and coffee, tea, and cocoa ($1.2 billion). It is interesting to note that foreign countries often sell products to the United States which are similar to those which the United States ships abroad —machinery and automobiles, for example.

The United States is becoming more dependent on foreign countries for some essential raw materials, such as copper, lead, zinc, and oil. This dependence seems certain to continue to grow in the future.

Changing needs

Substitutes are often developed for imported materials as a way of making the country more self-sufficient. Thus, silk once was a major import, until the development of synthetic fibers. And the nation's imports of raw rubber have dropped about 50 per cent in the last decade, as U. S. synthetic rubber factories increased their output. Between 1950 and 1962, American imports of apparel and carpet wool fell by half, as other fibers moved into the wool market. Tin imports dropped almost 60 per cent, a result of more efficient methods of using tin and also of competition from new materials. Broadening use of aluminum has lessened somewhat the need for foreign copper.

DESTINATION OF EXPORTS, 1962 (billions)

The most significant trend in exports in recent years has been the increasing proportion of the total that is sold to Western Europe.

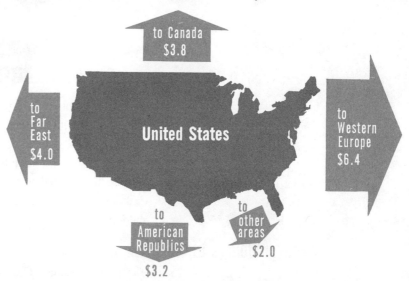

Changing customers and suppliers

Both foreign customers and foreign suppliers change over the years, as a look at the trade picture shows.

In 1953, U. S. exports were about equally divided among Canada, Latin America, Western Europe, and the rest of the world where U. S.

121

goods were sold. But nine years later, things were considerably different. The biggest U. S. customer in 1962 was Western Europe, which bought 35 per cent of all U. S. exports. Canada's purchases had dropped to 19 per cent of the total. Latin America's share was down to 16 per cent. To the rest of the world went the remaining 30 per cent of U. S. exports.

What about the goods bought abroad? In 1953, Latin America supplied 33 per cent of U. S. imports; nine years later, only 21 per cent. In those nine years Western Europe's share went up, from 21 per cent to 28 per cent. Canada's share—about one fifth—remained practically unchanged. And the United States was buying a larger percentage from the rest of the world in 1962 that it had bought a decade earlier. It spent $4.7 billion in 1962 for imported commodities in areas other than Western Europe, Canada, or Latin America. The purchases exceeded by $200 million those made in Western Europe. Nevertheless, Western Europe had emerged in less than 10 years as a major area of trade growth and potential for the United States.

Western Europe and Canada supply most of this country's imports of finished goods. Latin America is a major source of coffee, sugar, bananas, and other food imports.

ORIGIN OF IMPORTS, 1962 (billions)

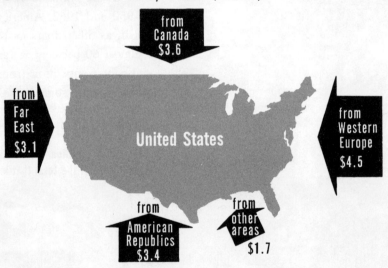

In order to buy from the United States, foreign countries must have the dollars with which to pay for their purchases. In part, they get them by their sales to U. S. customers. Even so, they don't sell enough merchandise here, and they haven't for many years. In 1950, for example, the United States sold $1.4 billion more in goods abroad than it bought. In 1957, the figure was $7.7 billion. In 1962, it was $5.1 billion.

Enough dollars to buy ? On the face of it, foreign countries were in trouble in their trade with the United States. They were going in debt to the tune of billions of dollars in order to make purchases in this country. Actually, their situation was by no means as bad as it seemed.

Since 1945, the United States has given and loaned $90 billion to other nations. Much of this money was for economic reconstruction. Billions also went for military aid. While the amount has been drop-

122

ping gradually, in 1962 it still totaled $4.5 billion—$2.8 billion for economic aid and $1.6 billion for military support. Until a few years ago, Western Europe was the major recipient of this aid. By 1963, most of it went to countries in the Near East, South Asia, the Far East, and the Pacific area. The amount going to Latin America— around $600 million a year—has also been increasing. With these loans and grants, foreign countries have been able to make purchases in the United States.

The "invisibles" The "invisibles"—the money going abroad from this country to pay travelers' expenses, interest and dividends to foreign investors, shipping costs on foreign carriers, foreign insurance bills, etc.—also helps foreign countries pay for their purchases here. These invisibles amount to billions of dollars every year. But, of course, the United States also gets income from foreigners who travel here or who borrow money here or who use U. S. ships for freight. The United States now pays out more than it takes in for everything but income on investments.

Thus, in 1962, American travelers spent $1 billion more for travel services abroad than foreign travelers spent in the United States. In addition, American shippers paid $300 million more to foreign transport services than the foreign shippers paid for similar services in this country. On the other hand, foreign investments returned to American investors $3.3 billion more in dividends and other income in 1962 than foreign investors received from their U. S. investments.

U. S. INTERNATIONAL TRADE AND FINANCE, 1962

America has been sending billions of dollars more abroad than it has received in recent years, due primarily to the amounts spent on foreign aid and the large U.S. investments in foreign industries. This has resulted in concern over what might happen to America's gold reserves if the trend is not corrected.

(billions)

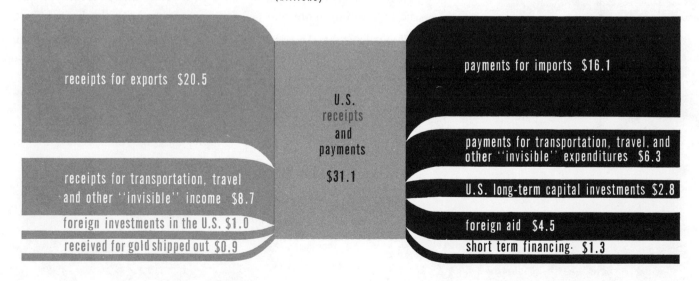

receipts for exports $20.5

receipts for transportation, travel and other "invisible" income $8.7

foreign investments in the U.S. $1.0

received for gold shipped out $0.9

U.S. receipts and payments $31.1

payments for imports $16.1

payments for transportation, travel, and other "invisible" expenditures $6.3

U.S. long-term capital investments $2.8

foreign aid $4.5

short term financing $1.3

Investment overseas U. S. investors have been investing heavily in stocks of foreign companies and in plants, factories, and other property abroad. In 1950, the net value of such investments (i.e., U. S. investments abroad less investments by foreigners in the United States) totaled not quite $14 billion. Twelve years later it amounted to about two and a half times as much, or nearly $33 billion. In other words, the net value of American investments abroad, both short-term and long-term, has been growing at a rate of slightly under $2 billion a year. For the year 1962, it was nearly $4 billion. The U. S.–financed oil refinery in Venezuela, the American–owned textile factory in Ireland, the supermarket in Italy, the machine plant in France—these are examples of how this money is put to work in other countries.

Result — the balance-of-payments deficit

Despite its success in selling goods overseas, the United States has not been able to maintain a balance between what it receives for exports and what it spends for imports, "invisibles," foreign aid, and foreign investments. In 1960, mostly because of its aid program and investments abroad, the country spent or gave away nearly $4 billion more than it received. In 1961, this deficit came to about $2.5 billion. In 1962, it dropped slightly to $2.2 billion.

Threat to the gold supply?

Many people regard this as a threat to the nation's gold supply, since the difference between what goes out and what is received would have to be made up in gold if customers abroad should insist. The drain cannot be kept up indefinitely. Reducing the deficit has become a major goal of U. S. foreign trade policy.

The course of future trade between the United States and the rest of the world depends on several factors. Easing the drain on America's gold supply is one of the most important. Mutual reduction of tariff barriers, particularly between the United States and the Common Market, could bring a greater volume of trade. On the other hand, should these barriers be raised, trade could be discouraged. Such a development might particularly damage U. S. agriculture.

Another trend to watch is the progress of the new, underdeveloped nations. Many, with the help of American loans, are gradually building up their industries and economies. In a few years, they will probably be able to buy more and sell more in trading with the United States.

The volume of America's foreign trade has grown somewhat faster than anticipated in recent years. It is very probable that this stepped-up pace will be maintained in the decade or so ahead.

CHAPTER XXI

The American Future

THE THOUGHTFUL AMERICAN CITIZEN, surveying the country in which he dwells, is compelled to ask: "What of tomorrow? What does the future hold for this nation of ours?"

The record of the past is clear and convincing. Out of the wealth of its resources and the skills of its people, the country has brought to fulfillment many of the dreams of men through the ages. Its democratic ways have set the course for a nation where freedom and liberty prevail. Its technological magic has made possible a productive plant able to satisfy whatever demands are made on it.

Together, this political democracy and technical genius have given the nation's almost 200 million citizens a way of life that is aspired to by the rest of the world.

Pressures and problems

Not without difficulty has the United States emerged to its present state of affluence and dynamic growth. There is always the fear that recession or worse might mar the happy picture. Maintaining employment for all who want jobs has been a constant challenge, not always successfully met. Adapting the economy to new methods of production and new ways of distribution will never be smooth nor simple.

There have been other problems, too—the rising cost of government, for one. Both at the national level and at state and local levels, a constant struggle is waged to limit government spending. But the cost of government continues to rise, as more is spent for national defense, for social welfare, and for the many services demanded by an increasingly urban society.

125

Meeting the nation's educational requirements has put severe pressures on schools, teachers, and parents. Only through unceasing effort have educators been able to keep up with the great influx of pupils into elementary schools, high schools, and now the colleges.

In the area of community relations, no challenge has been so difficult for all concerned as the securing of equal rights for 20 million Negro citizens. The problem has called for all the courage and judgment and patience of the country's national and local leaders, both Negro and white.

Poverty is still the lot of millions. One out of five families has an income of less than $3,000 a year. Of all the obstacles to the economy's growth, this is the most formidable and most disturbing.

AVERAGE INCOME PER FAMILY AFTER TAXES

In 33 years—1929 to 1962—average family income after taxes increased about 50 per cent. It will rise another 40 per cent by 1975.

(in 1960 dollars)

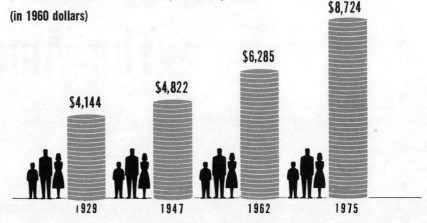

| $4,144 | $4,822 | $6,285 | $8,724 |
| 1929 | 1947 | 1962 | 1975 |

And, of course, never in its history has the country been so deeply involved in world relations and responsibilities. Its obligations abroad have required the expenditure of billions of dollars. It is committed to the encouragement and maintenance of democratic institutions and governments in many areas of the world. Together with its allies, particularly those of Western Europe, the United States has assumed responsibility for preserving and strengthening ways of life comparable to its own.

Foundations for tomorrow The future looks bright. Growth is assured, barring human catastrophe or miscalculation.

What are the ingredients of growth ahead? In summary, they include the following:

● Population. It is estimated that by 1975 the nation will have around 235 million people. While total population is expected to increase about 25 per cent over mid-1963, the growth among the younger age groups will be much greater. In the 20-to-34 age group, the increase will be closer to 40 per cent. These are the marrying ages, and it is the young people in this group who will set up households, have families, and buy unprecedented quantities of furniture, appliances, cars, clothing. They provide a vital market for U. S. business and industry.

● Technical advances. Today, according to the National Industrial Conference Board, almost one third of the nation's scientists and engineers are involved in laboratory research and development. Over $17 billion a year goes into this work, 25 times the sum spent 20 years ago. From this research have already come such basic new developments as nuclear energy, supersonic airplanes, transistors, thermoelectric refrigerators, miniaturized electronic products, and synthetic drugs, as well as new types of plastic materials and new foods, fuels, and textile fibers.

● Rising incomes. About one out of five families now has an income of $10,000 or more a year. By 1975, it is estimated that about two out of five families will have attained this level. Average annual family income is expected to be $9,525, compared with $7,011 in 1962. (These estimates are expressed in 1960 dollars.) As incomes rise, people will be able to buy more goods, to travel, to spend for education, to enjoy their leisure hours, and to move up the economic ladder. This kind of growth provides the propelling power of a dynamic economy. The prospect is that Americans a decade or so from now will be considerably better off than they are today.

● Increasing world trade. The nations with advanced economies, as well as those whose economies are only now developing, provide growing markets for U. S. goods, just as they are sources of supplies for products U. S. consumers seek abroad. This exchange of goods is important to the United States and to all its trading partners.

Fruits of growth In the years ahead, it is expected that trade between the United States and the rest of the world will grow significantly. By 1975, exports may reach $35 billion, compared with $20 billion in 1962. Imports may reach $29 billion, compared with $16.5 billion in 1962. (Again, the estimates are expressed in 1960 dollars.)

WHERE DO WE GO FROM HERE?

The nation's economy heads into a bright future. By 1975, industrial production is expected to be more than double the output of 1960. And gross national product will be approaching a trillion dollars a year (in 1960 dollars).

Industrial Production

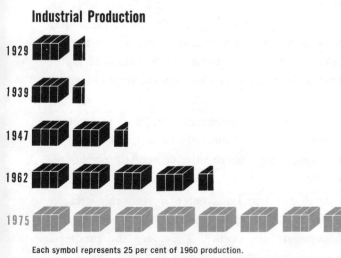

Each symbol represents 25 per cent of 1960 production.

Gross National Product

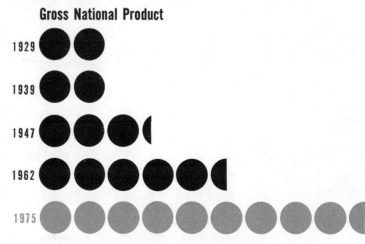

Each symbol represents 100 billion dollars, in 1960 prices.

The net result of these basic components of economic growth can be measured in many ways.

Gross national product is one index. In 1963, GNP was about $580 billion, or $561 billion in 1960 dollars. By 1975, if present growth rates continue, it will reach nearly $960 billion (in 1960 dollars).

Another measurement is personal income—the amount of money Americans have to spend, whether for taxes or for living expenses. In 1963 personal income was $463 billion, or $449 billion in 1960 dollars. In 1975, it is likely to be about $729 billion (in 1960 dollars).

Industrial production is still another measure of the economy's present and future strength. In 1963, the index (based on 1960 being equal to 100) was 114, or 2.8 times as high as the index for 1940. By 1975, it will probably approximate 212, or more than twice the 1960 index.

Productivity is the key

But the vitality of the American economy will, in the final analysis, depend on the same fundamental factor that brought it to its present dimensions: rising productivity.

Since 1947, the nation's productivity, in terms of GNP per worker, has increased slowly—about 2.3 per cent a year. But in the latter half of the sixties and in the seventies, it is probable that it will move ahead at a somewhat faster rate—about 2.6 per cent a year in the decade to come.

Opportunity of tomorrow

By the early seventies, Americans may well be moving into a new economic era. Space frontiers will be pierced and astronauts will probably have landed on the moon. No doubt, the pace of life will be faster and the opportunities more widespread. Interdependence with other nations will be greater, and America will share with all nations the responsibilities for world advancement.

In particular, America will strengthen her commercial, cultural, and political ties with the other nations in the North Atlantic region. It will be an extension of her present commitments as a member of the North Atlantic Treaty Organization and of the Organisation for Economic Cooperation and Development—the military and economic arms, respectively, of the United States, Western Europe, and other Western nations.

Across the Atlantic, the countries of Western Europe will probably continue their present trend toward integration, which began with the customs union of the Benelux countries (Belgium, the Netherlands, and Luxembourg) and which now finds its strongest expression in the organization of the European Economic Community or "Common Market," to which are affiliated as members the Benelux countries, West Germany, France, and Italy.

Staunch believers in the essential community of interest of the nations of the North Atlantic region feel that ultimately these trends will produce greater cooperation and unity between the democratic powers on both sides of the Atlantic.

However the future develops, Americans enter it with the strength that comes from the assurance of great assets. Their traditions are deep. Their past achievements are worthy. They face the problems ahead with neither fear nor indifference. Barring war or national disaster, responsible Americans believe that perhaps for the first time in its history the United States will have the energy and the resources to erase its shortcomings and to build the kind of nation that was dreamed of by the men who originally created it.

Appendix

The following tables present data on some of the more important aspects of American life and on the performance of the economy. They are designed to help the reader understand the trends discussed in Chapters I through XXI.

For simplification, the tables do not include footnotes and source notes. For refinements of the figures and modifications, such as whether or not the data shown are preliminary, are estimated, or are based on samples, consult the sources, a list of which is given on page 147.

POPULATION

America's population today is six times as large as it was a century ago and more than twice as large as in 1910.

The United States has become more and more a nation of city dwellers, with 7 out of 10 people living in urban areas today, compared with 4 out of 10 in 1900 and only 2 out of 10 just before the Civil War began.

As the country has grown, the population has become "older," i.e., has included a larger proportion of older people. The median age of the American people today is close to 29 years, compared with about 20 a century ago. There has been at least a temporary reversal in this "aging trend" since World War II. Only 25 per cent of the population was under 15 years of age in 1940, but this proportion has since risen to 31 per cent and promises to rise further in the years ahead. As a result, the median age has declined since 1950 and is expected to decline further.

The number of "senior citizens," on the other hand, has continued its steady climb, with more than 9 per cent of the population 65 years of age and over, compared with 2.5 per cent a century ago. This trend also seems likely to continue.

		per cent of total ...		in each age group ...			
year	total, thousands	living in urban areas	nonwhite	under 15	15–64	65 and over	median age
1790	3,929	5.1	19.3	n.a.	n.a.	n.a.	n.a.
1800	5,308	6.1	18.9	n.a.	n.a.	n.a.	16.0
1810	7,240	7.3	19.0	n.a.	n.a.	n.a.	16.0
1820	9,638	7.2	18.4	n.a.	n.a.	n.a.	16.7
1830	12,866	8.8	18.1	n.a.	n.a.	n.a.	17.2
1840	17,069	10.8	16.8	n.a.	n.a.	n.a.	17.8
1850	23,192	15.3	15.7	41.5	55.9	2.6	18.9
1860	31,443	19.8	14.4	40.5	57.0	2.5	19.4
1870	39,818	24.9	13.8	38.0	59.1	2.9	20.2
1880	50,156	28.2	13.5	38.1	58.5	3.4	20.9
1890	62,948	35.1	12.5	35.3	60.9	3.8	22.0
1900	75,995	39.7	12.1	34.4	61.5	4.1	22.9
1910	91,972	45.7	11.1	32.1	63.6	4.3	24.1
1920	105,711	51.2	10.3	31.8	63.5	4.7	25.3
1930	122,775	56.2	10.2	29.4	65.2	5.4	26.4
1940	131,669	56.5	10.2	25.0	68.2	6.8	29.0
1950	151,326	64.0	10.7	26.8	65.1	8.1	30.2
1960	179,323	69.9	11.4	31.0	59.8	9.2	29.5
1961	183,742	n.a.	11.5	31.4	59.3	9.3	29.1
1962	186,591	n.a.	11.6	31.2	59.5	9.3	28.8
1963	189,280	n.a.	11.7	31.0	59.7	9.3	28.5
1970	214,200	72.1	—	31.6	59.0	9.4	26.3
1975	235,300	73.2	—	32.4	58.2	9.4	25.7

POPULATION CHANGES, BY STATE AND REGION, July 1950—July 1975

state and region	number, thousands ...				percentage distribution ...				percentage change	
	1950	1960	1970	1975	1950	1960	1970	1975	1950–1960	1960–1970
United States, total	151,863	179,983	214,222	235,275	100.00	100.00	100.00	100.00	18.52	19.02
New England	9,320	10,504	12,404	13,543	6.14	5.84	5.79	5.76	12.70	18.09
Maine	911	973	1,093	1,174	0.60	0.54	0.51	0.50	6.80	12.33
New Hampshire	531	607	707	748	0.35	0.34	0.33	0.32	14.31	16.47
Vermont	377	389	450	464	0.25	0.22	0.21	0.20	3.18	15.68
Massachusetts	4,690	5,142	6,212	6,863	3.09	2.86	2.90	2.92	9.64	20.81
Rhode Island	779	855	921	967	0.51	0.48	0.43	0.41	9.76	7.72
Connecticut	2,032	2,539	3,021	3,327	1.34	1.41	1.41	1.41	24.95	18.98
Middle Atlantic	30,289	34,276	40,251	43,904	19.94	19.04	18.79	18.66	13.16	17.44
New York	14,909	16,863	19,472	21,061	9.82	9.37	9.09	8.95	13.11	15.48
New Jersey	4,860	6,090	7,691	8,692	3.20	3.38	3.59	3.69	25.31	26.29
Pennsylvania	10,520	11,323	13,088	14,151	6.93	6.29	6.11	6.01	7.63	15.60
East North Central	30,575	36,300	43,252	47,502	20.13	20.17	20.19	20.19	18.72	19.15
Ohio	7,998	9,743	11,654	12,825	5.27	5.41	5.44	5.45	21.82	19.61
Indiana	3,952	4,667	5,613	6,182	2.60	2.59	2.62	2.63	18.09	20.27
Illinois	8,754	10,077	12,061	13,299	5.76	5.60	5.63	5.65	15.11	19.69
Michigan	6,421	7,854	9,190	9,988	4.23	4.36	4.29	4.25	22.32	17.01
Wisconsin	3,449	3,959	4,734	5,208	2.27	2.20	2.21	2.21	14.79	19.58
West North Central	14,070	15,417	17,653	19,048	9.26	8.57	8.24	8.10	9.57	14.50
Minnesota	2,995	3,421	4,199	4,679	1.97	1.90	1.96	1.99	14.22	22.74
Iowa	2,621	2,762	3,149	3,382	1.73	1.53	1.47	1.44	5.38	14.01
Missouri	3,946	4,322	4,927	5,289	2.60	2.40	2.30	2.25	9.53	14.00
North Dakota	616	634	643	655	0.41	0.35	0.30	0.28	2.92	1.42
South Dakota	652	684	686	706	0.43	0.38	0.32	0.30	4.91	0.29
Nebraska	1,324	1,415	1,564	1,647	0.87	0.79	0.73	0.70	6.87	10.53
Kansas	1,915	2,180	2,485	2,690	1.26	1.21	1.16	1.14	13.84	13.99
South Atlantic	21,230	26,087	31,320	34,496	13.98	14.49	14.62	14.66	22.88	20.06
Delaware	321	449	600	705	0.21	0.25	0.28	0.30	39.88	33.63
Maryland	2,376	3,108	4,049	4,640	1.56	1.73	1.89	1.97	30.81	30.28
District of Columbia	814	767	857	903	0.54	0.43	0.40	0.38	−5.77	11.73
Virginia	3,262	3,988	4,777	5,235	2.15	2.22	2.23	2.23	22.26	19.78
West Virginia	2,006	1,850	2,014	2,088	1.32	1.03	0.94	0.89	−7.78	8.86
North Carolina	4,060	4,572	5,077	5,379	2.67	2.54	2.37	2.29	12.61	11.04
South Carolina	2,119	2,393	2,614	2,751	1.40	1.33	1.22	1.17	12.93	9.24
Georgia	3,451	3,956	4,734	5,192	2.27	2.20	2.21	2.21	14.63	19.67
Florida	2,821	5,004	6,598	7,603	1.86	2.78	3.08	3.23	77.38	31.85
East South Central	11,490	12,074	13,710	14,718	7.57	6.71	6.40	6.26	5.08	13.55
Kentucky	2,957	3,042	3,492	3,764	1.95	1.69	1.63	1.60	2.87	14.79
Tennessee	3,304	3,572	4,134	4,482	2.18	1.98	1.93	1.90	8.11	15.73
Alabama	3,060	3,276	3,706	3,970	2.01	1.82	1.73	1.69	7.06	13.13
Mississippi	2,169	2,184	2,378	2,502	1.43	1.21	1.11	1.06	0.69	8.88
West South Central	14,548	17,036	20,500	22,621	9.58	9.47	9.57	9.61	17.10	20.34
Arkansas	1,906	1,789	1,907	1,987	1.26	0.99	0.89	0.84	−6.14	6.60
Louisiana	2,701	3,265	4,027	4,495	1.78	1.81	1.88	1.91	20.88	23.34
Oklahoma	2,193	2,339	2,635	2,803	1.44	1.30	1.23	1.19	6.66	12.65
Texas	7,748	9,643	11,931	13,336	5.10	5.36	5.57	5.67	24.46	23.74
Mountain	5,120	6,927	8,590	9,628	3.37	3.85	4.01	4.09	35.29	24.01
Montana	598	680	771	836	0.39	0.38	0.36	0.36	13.71	13.38
Idaho	592	671	771	831	0.39	0.37	0.36	0.35	13.34	14.90
Wyoming	292	332	364	384	0.19	0.18	0.17	0.16	13.70	9.64
Colorado	1,337	1,769	2,228	2,516	0.88	0.98	1.04	1.07	32.31	25.95
New Mexico	687	958	1,242	1,440	0.45	0.53	0.58	0.61	39.45	29.64
Arizona	756	1,325	1,757	2,017	0.50	0.74	0.82	0.86	75.26	32.60
Utah	696	901	1,050	1,140	0.46	0.50	0.49	0.48	29.45	16.54
Nevada	162	291	407	464	0.13	0.16	0.19	0.20	79.63	39.86
Pacific	15,220	21,363	26,542	29,815	10.02	11.87	12.39	12.67	40.36	24.25
Washington	2,386	2,868	3,385	3,724	1.57	1.59	1.58	1.58	20.20	18.03
Oregon	1,532	1,770	2,142	2,374	1.01	0.98	1.00	1.01	15.54	21.02
California	10,674	15,855	19,922	22,467	7.03	8.81	9.30	9.55	48.54	25.66
Alaska	138	228	343	429	0.09	0.13	0.16	0.18	65.22	50.44
Hawaii	491	642	750	821	0.32	0.36	0.35	0.35	30.75	16.82

BIRTHS AND DEATHS

year	births per thousand population	deaths ... per thousand population	per thousand live births ... mothers	per thousand live births ... infants	life expectancy at birth, years ... male	life expectancy at birth, years ... female
1900	32.3	17.2	n.a.	n.a.	46.3	48.3
1905	n.a.	15.9	n.a.	n.a.	47.3	50.2
1910	30.1	14.7	n.a.	n.a.	48.4	51.8
1915	29.5	13.2	6.1	99.9	52.5	56.8
1920	27.7	13.0	8.0	85.8	53.6	54.6
1925	25.1	11.7	6.5	71.7	57.6	60.6
1930	21.3	11.3	6.7	64.6	58.1	61.6
1935	18.7	10.9	5.8	55.7	59.9	63.9
1940	19.4	10.8	3.8	47.0	60.8	65.2
1945	20.4	10.6	2.1	38.3	63.6	67.9
1950	24.1	9.6	0.8	29.2	65.6	71.1
1955	25.0	9.3	0.5	26.4	66.6	72.7
1956	25.2	9.4	0.4	26.0	66.7	73.0
1957	25.3	9.6	0.4	26.3	66.3	72.5
1958	24.6	9.5	0.4	27.1	66.4	72.7
1959	24.3	9.4	0.4	26.4	66.5	73.0
1960	23.7	9.5	0.4	26.0	66.6	73.1
1961	23.3	9.3	0.4	25.3	n.a.	n.a.
1962	22.4	9.5	0.3	25.3	n.a.	n.a.

The birth rate is much lower today than in the early 1900s, but it is still considerably higher than the low point reached in the depression of the 1930s.

Death rates have fallen substantially since 1900. Deaths have averaged around 9.5 per thousand people annually over the past several years. The sharp drop in infant deaths to a quarter of the 1915 infant mortality rate has been the biggest factor in the decline.

The result of these trends has been a substantial rise in life expectancy. Newborn girls, on the average, can expect to reach an age of 73 compared with 48 in 1900. Life expectancy of baby boys has risen from 46 years to over 66 years.

Population growth was more than twice as fast in the Pacific states as in the country as a whole from 1950 to 1960. In the Rocky Mountain states, growth was almost twice the national rate. The fastest growing states in recent years have been Florida, California, Delaware, Arizona, Alaska, Nevada, and New Mexico.

HOUSEHOLDS AND CONSUMER UNITS

year	total persons in households, millions	households, millions	persons per household	consumer units, millions
1929	121.8	29.6	4.1	36.1
1930	123.1	30.0	4.1	n.a.
1935	127.2	31.9	4.0	n.a.
1940	132.5	35.2	3.8	n.a.
1941	133.7	35.9	3.7	41.4
1942	134.6	36.4	3.7	n.a.
1943	135.1	36.8	3.7	n.a.
1944	133.9	37.1	3.6	40.9
1945	133.4	37.5	3.6	n.a.
1946	140.7	38.4	3.7	43.3
1947	144.1	39.4	3.7	44.7
1948	146.7	40.9	3.6	46.3
1949	149.3	42.5	3.5	47.8
1950	151.9	43.8	3.5	48.9
1951	154.0	44.8	3.4	49.5
1952	156.4	45.7	3.4	50.2
1953	159.0	46.5	3.4	50.5
1954	161.9	47.1	3.4	51.2
1955	165.1	48.0	3.4	52.2
1956	168.1	49.0	3.4	52.8
1957	171.2	49.8	3.4	53.6
1958	174.1	50.7	3.4	54.6
1959	177.1	51.6	3.4	55.3
1960	180.0	52.6	3.4	56.1
1961	183.0	53.3	3.4	57.3
1962	185.0	54.7	3.4	58.6
1970	213.0	62.0	3.4	—
1975	234.0	68.0	3.4	—

In 1962, there were 47 million families and about 11.5 million unattached persons in the United States; 7.5 million of the latter group lived alone, and thus were classified as one-person households.

As defined by the Census Bureau, a "household" includes all persons who occupy a housing unit—a house, an apartment, or other group of rooms, or a room that constitutes separate living quarters. Such persons may or may not make up a "family," which consists of two or more persons who live together and who are related by blood, marriage, or adoption. Persons living alone are listed as households but not as families in census counts.

"Consumer units" include all families and unattached individuals. The number of consumer units exceeds the number of households, because many unattached individuals who do not maintain separate households—for example, those living in rooming houses—are counted as consumer units.

The decline in the average size of the household since the early 1930s reflects the fact that there is less "doubling up" of families, fewer boarders in private households, and a growing tendency for older children to leave the family and set up their own households before marriage.

THE LABOR FORCE

year	total as per cent of population 14 years of age and over	number, millions ...		members of armed forces	civilian ...	
		total	civilian		per cent unemployed	per cent female
1929	n.a.	49.4	49.2	0.3	3.2	n.a.
1930	n.a.	50.1	49.8	0.3	8.7	n.a.
1931	n.a.	50.7	50.4	0.3	15.9	n.a.
1932	n.a.	51.2	51.0	0.2	23.6	n.a.
1933	n.a.	51.8	51.6	0.2	24.9	n.a.
1934	n.a.	52.5	52.2	0.3	21.7	n.a.
1935	n.a.	53.1	52.9	0.3	20.1	n.a.
1936	n.a.	53.7	53.4	0.3	16.9	n.a.
1937	n.a.	54.3	54.0	0.3	14.3	n.a.
1938	n.a.	55.0	54.6	0.3	19.0	n.a.
1939	n.a.	55.6	55.2	0.4	17.2	n.a.
1940	56.0	56.2	55.6	0.5	14.6	25.4
1941	56.7	57.5	55.9	1.6	9.9	26.2
1942	58.8	60.4	56.4	4.0	4.7	28.6
1943	62.3	64.6	55.5	9.0	1.9	33.7
1944	63.1	66.0	54.6	11.4	1.2	35.1
1945	61.9	65.3	53.9	11.4	1.9	35.3
1946	57.2	61.0	57.5	3.4	3.9	29.3
1947	57.4	61.8	60.2	1.6	3.9	28.1
1948	57.9	62.9	61.4	1.5	3.8	28.6
1949	58.0	63.7	62.1	1.6	5.9	29.0
1950	58.4	64.7	63.1	1.6	5.3	29.6
1951	58.9	66.0	62.9	3.1	3.3	30.6
1952	58.8	66.6	63.0	3.6	3.1	31.0
1953	58.5	67.4	63.8	3.5	2.9	30.7
1954	58.4	67.8	64.5	3.4	5.6	30.9
1955	58.7	68.9	65.8	3.0	4.4	31.6
1956	59.3	70.4	67.5	2.9	4.2	32.2
1957	58.7	70.7	67.9	2.8	4.3	32.5
1958	58.5	71.3	68.6	2.6	6.8	32.7
1959	58.3	71.9	69.4	2.6	5.5	32.9
1960	58.3	73.1	70.6	2.5	5.6	33.4
1961	58.0	74.2	71.6	2.6	6.7	33.8
1962	57.4	74.7	71.9	2.8	5.6	34.1
1970	57.0	85.8	83.3	2.5	4.0	35.6
1975	57.0	93.0	90.7	2.3	4.0	35.8

Except for the increased proportion during World War II, the labor force has remained at a fairly stable 57 to 59 per cent of the population over 14 years of age.

Women constitute a larger proportion of the civilian labor force today than at any previous time, except at the peak of World War II. They are more than a third of the total, compared with a quarter in 1940.

Although unemployment is much lower than in the long depression of the 1930s, it has remained at more than 5 per cent of the civilian labor force in recent years.

Per Cent of Civilian Labor Force Unemployed

1947   1952   1957   1962

year	number, millions ...					factory workers as per cent of all nonfarm workers	average weekly hours of all nonfarm wage and salary workers	average weekly earnings of wage workers in manufacturing ...			cost-of-living index (1960=100)	fringe benefits as per cent of wages and salaries in manufacturing
		working for ...		all nonfarm wage and salary workers	factory workers only			in current prices	real wages ...			
	total	government	private employers						in 1960 prices	index (1960=100)		
1929	47.6	3.1	44.6	31.3	8.6	27.3	44.5	$24.76	$42.76	47.7	57.9	0.9
1930	45.5	3.1	42.3	29.4	7.5	25.4	43.2	23.00	40.74	45.4	56.5	1.0
1931	42.4	3.3	39.1	26.6	6.3	23.6	n.a.	20.64	40.14	44.7	51.4	1.1
1932	38.9	3.2	35.7	23.6	5.4	22.6	n.a.	16.89	36.60	40.8	46.2	1.4
1933	38.8	3.2	35.6	23.7	5.9	25.0	n.a.	16.65	38.08	42.4	43.7	1.2
1934	40.9	3.3	37.6	26.0	6.9	26.6	n.a.	18.20	42.24	47.1	45.2	1.1
1935	42.3	3.5	38.8	27.1	7.4	27.3	n.a.	19.91	42.93	47.3	46.4	1.2
1936	44.4	3.7	40.7	29.1	8.0	27.6	n.a.	21.56	46.02	51.3	46.8	2.1
1937	46.3	3.8	42.5	31.0	8.8	28.3	n.a.	23.82	49.08	54.7	48.5	4.2
1938	44.2	3.9	40.3	29.2	7.5	25.6	n.a.	22.07	46.37	51.7	47.6	5.5
1939	45.8	4.0	41.8	30.6	8.3	27.2	n.a.	23.64	50.34	56.1	46.9	5.4
1940	47.5	4.2	43.3	32.4	8.9	27.6	41.1	24.96	52.76	58.8	47.3	5.2
1941	50.4	4.7	45.7	36.6	11.0	30.1	43.2	29.48	59.27	66.1	49.8	4.9
1942	53.8	5.5	48.3	40.1	13.0	32.4	44.3	36.68	66.61	74.2	55.1	4.3
1943	54.5	6.1	48.4	42.5	15.1	35.7	46.4	43.07	73.64	82.1	58.5	4.3
1944	54.0	6.0	47.9	41.9	14.7	35.2	46.2	45.70	76.85	85.7	59.5	4.8
1945	52.8	5.9	46.9	40.4	13.0	32.2	45.0	44.20	72.71	81.0	60.8	5.1
1946	55.2	5.6	49.6	41.7	12.3	29.5	43.0	43.32	65.68	73.2	66.0	4.7
1947	57.8	5.5	52.3	43.9	13.0	29.6	42.3	49.17	65.18	72.6	75.5	4.8
1948	59.1	5.6	53.5	44.9	12.9	28.8	41.6	53.12	65.33	72.8	81.3	4.6
1949	58.4	5.9	52.6	43.8	11.8	26.9	40.9	53.83	66.94	74.6	80.5	5.2
1950	59.7	6.0	53.7	45.2	12.5	27.7	40.7	58.32	71.74	80.0	81.3	6.4
1951	60.8	6.4	54.4	47.8	13.4	27.9	41.3	63.34	72.15	80.4	87.8	7.1
1952	61.0	6.6	54.4	48.8	13.4	27.4	41.6	67.16	74.88	83.5	89.7	7.0
1953	61.9	6.6	55.3	50.2	14.1	28.0	41.1	70.47	77.96	86.9	90.4	7.1
1954	60.9	6.8	54.1	49.0	12.8	26.1	40.0	70.49	77.65	86.5	90.8	7.6
1955	62.9	6.9	56.0	50.7	13.3	26.2	40.9	75.70	83.64	93.2	90.5	7.9
1956	64.7	7.3	57.4	52.4	13.4	25.6	40.9	78.78	85.78	95.6	91.9	8.2
1957	65.0	7.6	57.4	52.9	13.2	24.9	40.5	81.59	85.81	95.6	95.1	8.9
1958	64.0	7.9	56.1	51.4	12.0	23.3	40.1	82.71	84.67	94.4	97.7	9.2
1959	65.6	8.2	57.4	53.4	12.6	23.6	40.0	88.26	89.67	99.9	98.4	9.7
1960	66.7	8.5	58.2	54.4	12.6	23.2	40.0	89.72	89.72	100.0	100.0	10.2
1961	66.8	8.8	58.0	54.2	12.1	22.3	40.1	92.34	91.39	101.9	101.1	10.4
1962	67.8	9.2	58.7	55.8	12.5	22.4	40.0	96.56	94.48	105.3	102.2	10.7
1970	80.0	11.5	68.5	—	—	—	37.8	—	—	—	—	—
1975	87.1	12.8	74.3	—	—	—	37.0	—	—	—	—	—

One out of eight civilian workers is employed by government—federal, state or local.

Of the more than 9 million government employees, nearly 7 million work for state and local governments. Half of the 7 million are employed by public school systems.

The number of factory ("blue-collar") workers is about the same today as in 1946, but the number of white-collar workers has increased about 50 per cent since then. More than a third of all nonfarm wage and salary workers were employed in factories during World War II. Today little more than one fifth work in factories.

Americans today work an average of 40 hours per week; Western Europeans close to 45 hours.

The average factory worker today gets about four times as many dollars in his weekly pay envelope as he did in 1929, and almost six times as many as at the bottom of the depression in 1933. But prices and the cost of

living have also been rising, though not as steeply as wages.

The result is that average "real wages" of factory workers, measured in terms of 1960 purchasing power, were about $43 per week in 1929, less than $37 in 1932, and about $95 in 1962.

Major fringe benefits, mainly employer contributions for social insurance and to private pension, health, and welfare funds, add more than 10 per cent to cash earnings today—about ten times the proportion they represented thirty years ago.

PRODUCTIVITY

	GNP per person employed in 1960 prices	indexes: (1960=100)		
year		GNP per person employed	nonfarm private product per man-hour	output per man-hour in manufacturing
1929	$4,321	59.2	n.a.	n.a.
1933	3,691	50.6	n.a.	n.a.
1940	4,867	66.7	n.a.	n.a.
1944	5,750	78.8	n.a.	n.a.
1947	5,403	74.1	72.8	70.5
1948	5,501	75.4	74.3	72.4
1949	5,567	76.3	77.1	74.0
1950	5,904	80.9	81.1	78.9
1951	6,127	84.0	82.5	80.3
1952	6,293	86.3	83.6	81.5
1953	6,501	89.1	85.9	85.4
1954	6,481	88.8	87.2	84.7
1955	6,819	93.5	90.9	90.5
1956	6,790	93.1	90.5	91.5
1957	6,898	94.5	93.0	91.6
1958	6,911	94.7	94.8	93.2
1959	7,204	98.7	98.3	97.7
1960	7,296	100.0	100.0	100.0
1961	7,418	101.7	102.9	104.4
1962	7,643	104.8	106.9	108.3

Productivity, measured in terms of GNP per person employed, has risen more than 75 per cent since 1929, or at an annual compound rate of 1.7 per cent. This is a somewhat crude measure of the productivity of the total economy. Measures of the output per man-hour, as shown for the nonfarm private sector of the economy and for manufacturing alone, are more definitive measures of productivity.

Productivity in the nonfarm private sector of the economy has been rising at an annual compound rate of 2.6 per cent since 1947, but in manufacturing alone, the rise has been slightly larger—2.9 per cent.

Productivity Trends

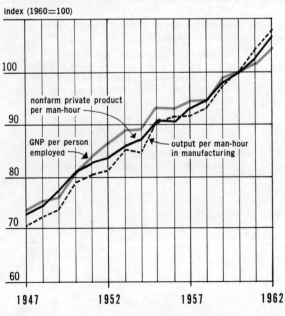

index (1960=100)

nonfarm private product per man-hour

GNP per person employed

output per man-hour in manufacturing

1947 1952 1957 1962

PRODUCTIVE CAPACITY

		value of industrial and commercial facilities, billions ...		
year	index of industrial production (1960=100)	in current prices	in 1960 prices	expenditures for nonfarm, nonresidential capital goods, billions
1929	35.0	$122.6	$329.1	$12.6
1930	29.4	n.a.	n.a.	10.9
1931	24.9	n.a.	n.a.	7.7
1932	19.3	n.a.	n.a.	4.6
1933	22.1	107.7	340.1	4.1
1934	24.9	n.a.	n.a.	5.3
1935	28.5	n.a.	n.a.	6.1
1936	33.1	n.a.	n.a.	8.7
1937	36.8	n.a.	n.a.	9.8
1938	28.5	n.a.	n.a.	8.4
1939	35.0	123.9	338.5	9.4
1940	40.5	n.a.	n.a.	10.7
1941	51.5	n.a.	n.a.	14.3
1942	63.5	n.a.	n.a.	10.5
1943	76.3	n.a.	n.a.	7.6
1944	75.4	n.a.	n.a.	8.1
1945	65.3	172.3	361.8	10.8
1946	55.2	214.2	371.7	17.4
1947	60.4	257.6	387.6	25.0
1948	62.9	286.1	406.1	29.7
1949	59.5	292.5	420.9	29.3
1950	68.9	328.6	437.8	31.7
1951	74.8	359.0	457.1	37.4
1952	77.5	383.8	475.6	39.1
1953	84.0	407.2	496.0	41.8
1954	78.9	429.8	515.1	42.0
1955	88.8	461.8	536.8	45.9
1956	91.9	510.6	562.8	53.0
1957	92.6	562.7	589.7	56.6
1958	86.2	593.2	609.3	50.1
1959	97.1	629.2	634.2	51.0
1960	100.0	660.3	660.3	56.3
1961	101.0	690.9	687.4	57.4
1962	108.8	726.7	715.6	61.1

The dollar value of industrial and commercial facilities in 1962 was about six times that of 1929, but when allowance is made for price changes, it becomes apparent that the real value of the country's productive capacity little more than doubled during the period.

The index of industrial production, which shows the trend in quantity of goods produced, was more than three times as high in 1962 as in 1929, and almost six times as high as in 1932, its low point in the depression.

More than $61 billion, about one ninth of total GNP, was invested during 1962 in new industrial plant and equipment, commercial facilities, and civilian government installations.

GROSS NATIONAL PRODUCT

year	total, billions, in current prices	in 1960 prices ... billions ... total	personal consumption expenditures	gross private domestic investment	government purchases of goods and services	net exports of goods and services	per capita ... total	personal consumption expenditures	gross private domestic investment	government purchases of goods and services as per cent of GNP
1929	$104	$207.6	$141.6	$41.7	$ 23.5	$0.8	$1,704	$1,163	$342	11.3
1930	91	187.7	132.7	28.2	26.0	0.8	1,524	1,077	229	13.8
1931	76	174.2	128.5	18.2	27.3	0.2	1,404	1,035	147	15.7
1932	58	148.4	116.8	5.5	26.0	0.1	1,188	935	44	17.5
1933	56	144.6	114.3	5.7	25.1	−0.5	1,150	909	45	17.4
1934	65	158.1	120.1	9.4	28.8	−0.2	1,250	949	74	18.2
1935	72	174.3	127.7	19.0	29.1	−1.5	1,368	1,002	149	16.7
1936	83	197.7	140.7	24.9	33.8	−1.7	1,542	1,098	194	17.1
1937	91	209.1	146.0	31.5	32.7	−1.1	1,621	1,132	244	15.6
1938	85	199.6	143.2	18.9	36.2	1.3	1,535	1,102	145	18.1
1939	91	216.3	151.6	25.8	38.0	0.9	1,651	1,157	197	17.6
1940	101	234.5	159.4	34.3	39.1	1.7	1,775	1,207	260	16.7
1941	126	272.6	170.3	43.0	59.4	−0.1	2,043	1,277	322	21.8
1942	159	309.9	166.4	22.1	123.9	−2.5	2,297	1,234	164	40.0
1943	192	347.9	170.6	13.1	170.3	−6.1	2,545	1,248	96	49.0
1944	211	373.2	176.5	15.1	187.9	−6.3	2,697	1,275	109	50.3
1945	214	367.0	189.0	20.9	162.0	−4.9	2,623	1,351	149	44.1
1946	211	321.6	212.0	50.1	54.8	4.7	2,274	1,496	354	17.0
1947	234	321.5	215.6	50.2	46.5	9.2	2,231	1,493	348	14.5
1948	259	334.6	219.9	59.3	52.6	2.8	2,282	1,496	404	15.7
1949	258	335.1	225.4	47.0	59.1	3.6	2,246	1,506	315	17.6
1950	285	362.6	238.7	66.2	56.6	1.1	2,390	1,572	436	15.6
1951	329	390.9	240.6	68.1	79.0	3.2	2,533	1,558	441	20.2
1952	347	406.4	247.0	60.4	96.8	2.2	2,590	1,573	385	23.8
1953	365	424.6	258.7	61.1	104.8	0.0	2,660	1,621	383	24.7
1954	363	417.1	262.1	59.1	93.9	2.0	2,568	1,614	364	22.5
1955	398	449.4	281.7	74.4	91.4	1.9	2,719	1,703	450	20.3
1956	419	459.0	291.2	73.7	90.3	3.8	2,729	1,729	438	19.7
1957	443	467.9	298.6	69.8	94.4	5.1	2,731	1,744	407	20.2
1958	444	459.8	300.7	59.1	99.1	0.9	2,639	1,730	339	21.6
1959	483	490.3	318.3	72.8	100.2	−1.0	2,768	1,801	411	20.4
1960	503	503.4	328.5	72.3	99.8	2.8	2,786	1,828	401	19.8
1961	518	512.6	335.1	69.2	105.1	3.2	2,790	1,825	377	20.5
1962	555	540.1	350.4	75.2	112.8	1.7	2,894	1,877	406	20.9
1970	—	780.0	472.0	124.7	181.0	2.3	3,641	2,204	582	23.2
1975	—	955.0	570.0	157.3	225.0	2.7	4,059	2,422	668	23.6

The American economy in 1962 turned out nearly four times the total volume of goods and services produced at the bottom of the depression, in 1933. (This is in 1960 purchasing power, which means that GNP for all years in current value has been converted to dollars of constant purchasing power by applying an index to eliminate price changes.)

About two thirds of total gross national product (or gross national expenditure) consists of goods and services bought by consumers for their own use.

Most of the remaining third of GNP consists of investment by individuals and business firms in houses, apartments and hotels, and in factories, machinery, and equipment used to produce other goods and services; and of purchases of goods and services by local, state, and federal governments in conducting their normal activities. The government share of GNP amounted to more than half the total in the last year of World War II. It had fallen to 21 per cent by 1962.

American economic progress has been less spectacular than it appears, since population has been increasing steadily. Per capita GNP in 1962 (in 1960 prices) was only two and one half times that of 1933.

PERCENTAGE DISTRIBUTION OF GNP

One half or more of the total volume of goods and services produced by the national economy in recent years consisted of tangible, movable goods; about 11 per cent of bridges, roads, dwellings, factories, and other permanent structures; and the remainder of intangible services, such as transportation, radio broadcasting, teaching, police protection, and various personal services.

More than four fifths of the GNP originates with business firms, nearly half the remainder with government. The government share is primarily compensation of employees, including the armed forces, and is not the same as government purchases of goods and services (shown on p 135.), which also include government transactions with private business. The rest consists of the output of farms and households (including clubs and nonprofit organizations) and net income from abroad.

| | by type of product ... | | | | by sector or origin ... | | | | | |
year	total	goods	services	con-struction	total	nonfarm business	farm	govern-ment	household	rest of world
1929	100.0	53.9	35.4	10.7	100.0	81.4	9.4	4.1	4.3	0.8
1930	100.0	51.7	38.4	9.9	100.0	81.8	8.5	4.9	4.0	0.8
1931	100.0	49.0	42.2	8.6	100.0	81.0	8.1	6.2	3.9	0.7
1932	100.0	45.8	47.9	6.3	100.0	79.8	7.5	7.5	4.3	0.7
1933	100.0	48.4	46.6	5.0	100.0	78.8	8.2	8.4	3.9	0.5
1934	100.0	52.5	42.3	5.1	100.0	80.6	6.6	8.6	3.7	0.5
1935	100.0	55.0	39.6	5.4	100.0	78.3	9.5	8.1	3.4	0.6
1936	100.0	55.3	38.1	6.6	100.0	79.9	7.6	8.8	3.4	0.4
1937	100.0	56.6	36.2	7.3	100.0	79.7	8.9	7.6	3.4	0.3
1938	100.0	53.3	39.6	7.2	100.0	79.3	7.9	8.9	3.4	0.5
1939	100.0	54.0	37.9	8.1	100.0	80.8	7.1	8.3	3.4	0.3
1940	100.0	56.1	35.8	8.2	100.0	81.8	6.8	7.8	3.4	0.4
1941	100.0	58.2	32.5	9.2	100.0	82.0	7.5	7.5	2.9	0.3
1942	100.0	59.4	31.7	8.9	100.0	79.5	8.4	9.5	2.3	0.3
1943	100.0	63.0	32.5	4.5	100.0	76.6	7.9	13.3	2.0	0.2
1944	100.0	63.3	34.0	2.7	100.0	75.2	7.4	15.2	2.0	0.2
1945	100.0	61.2	35.9	2.9	100.0	73.5	7.6	16.5	2.2	0.2
1946	100.0	61.1	32.5	6.4	100.0	78.3	9.2	9.8	2.4	0.3
1947	100.0	61.4	30.6	8.0	100.0	81.1	8.8	7.1	2.6	0.3
1948	100.0	60.5	30.1	9.4	100.0	81.1	9.2	6.7	2.7	0.4
1949	100.0	57.8	32.4	9.8	100.0	81.8	7.5	7.5	2.9	0.4
1950	100.0	57.5	31.6	11.0	100.0	82.1	7.2	7.3	3.0	0.4
1951	100.0	58.3	31.3	10.4	100.0	81.4	7.2	8.3	2.8	0.4
1952	100.0	57.1	32.4	10.5	100.0	81.3	6.6	8.9	2.8	0.4
1953	100.0	56.6	32.7	10.7	100.0	82.2	5.7	8.7	3.0	0.4
1954	100.0	54.4	34.2	11.5	100.0	81.9	5.6	8.9	3.1	0.4
1955	100.0	54.6	33.6	11.8	100.0	82.9	4.9	8.6	3.2	0.5
1956	100.0	54.3	34.2	11.5	100.0	82.9	4.6	8.7	3.4	0.5
1957	100.0	53.8	34.9	11.3	100.0	82.9	4.4	8.8	3.5	0.5
1958	100.0	51.6	36.9	11.5	100.0	81.6	4.8	9.4	3.7	0.5
1959	100.0	51.9	36.4	11.7	100.0	82.6	4.1	9.1	3.6	0.5
1960	100.0	51.3	37.5	11.3	100.0	82.2	4.2	9.4	3.9	0.5
1961	100.0	50.0	38.7	11.3	100.0	81.6	4.1	9.8	3.9	0.6
1962	100.0	50.0	38.8	11.2	100.0	81.8	3.9	9.8	3.9	0.6

Distribution of GNP by Type of Product

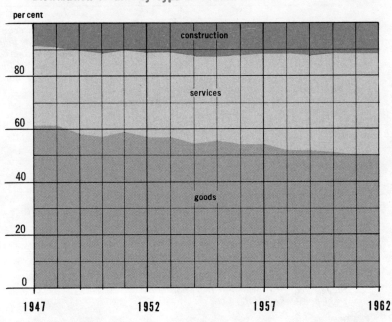

CORPORATE PROFITS

amounts in billions

year	before taxes	after taxes ... amount	as per cent of sales
1929	$9.6	$8.3	6.0
1930	3.3	2.5	2.1
1931	−0.8	−1.3	−1.4
1932	−3.0	−3.4	−4.9
1933	0.2	−0.4	−0.5
1934	1.7	1.0	1.1
1935	3.1	2.2	2.2
1936	5.7	4.3	3.6
1937	6.2	4.7	3.7
1938	3.3	2.3	2.1
1939	6.4	5.0	4.1
1940	9.3	6.5	4.8
1941	17.0	9.4	5.3
1942	20.9	9.5	4.7
1943	24.6	10.5	4.5
1944	23.3	10.4	4.2
1945	19.0	8.3	3.5
1946	22.6	13.4	5.0
1947	29.5	18.2	5.2
1948	33.0	20.5	5.3
1949	26.4	16.0	4.3
1950	40.6	22.8	5.3
1951	42.2	19.7	4.0
1952	36.7	17.2	3.4
1953	38.3	18.1	3.5
1954	34.1	16.8	3.3
1955	44.9	23.0	3.8
1956	44.7	23.5	3.7
1957	43.2	22.3	3.3
1958	37.4	18.8	2.9
1959	47.7	24.5	3.3
1960	44.3	22.0	2.9
1961	43.8	21.8	2.8
1962	46.8	24.6	3.0

Profits of American corporations were nearly five times as large in 1962 as in prosperous 1929. Profits after payment of taxes, however, were about three times as large.

During this 33-year period, moreover, costs and prices have just about doubled, so that the purchasing power of the 1962 dollar, in terms of capital investment and consumer buying power, was little more than half that of the earlier year. The 1962 profit ratio of three per cent of total corporate sales was only half that of 1929.

INCOME AND SAVINGS

1960 prices, billions

year	national income	personal income	disposable personal income	personal savings
1929	$175	$154	$149	$7.5
1930	156	144	139	6.4
1931	137	138	134	5.3
1932	108	119	115	−1.6
1933	104	116	113	−1.7
1934	120	124	120	0.3
1935	138	136	132	4.5
1936	156	154	149	8.1
1937	170	160	154	8.0
1938	159	152	146	2.5
1939	173	164	158	6.2
1940	191	174	169	9.3
1941	227	200	193	23.0
1942	264	229	218	51.6
1943	300	257	227	56.2
1944	314	266	236	59.5
1945	305	266	233	44.4
1946	278	258	231	19.4
1947	273	250	222	6.2
1948	289	259	233	13.5
1949	282	259	236	10.4
1950	307	280	254	15.5
1951	332	294	261	20.3
1952	341	307	268	21.2
1953	355	321	281	22.2
1954	346	319	283	20.8
1955	373	340	301	19.3
1956	383	359	316	24.8
1957	387	368	323	24.8
1958	380	370	326	25.5
1959	407	390	342	23.9
1960	416	401	349	20.9
1961	423	413	360	25.3
1962	447	433	376	25.7
1970	621	595	514	42.0
1975	759	729	626	56.0

National income in 1962 was more than four times as large, in dollars of constant purchasing power, as it was at the depth of the depression of the 1930s.

Disposable personal income, which represents the amount remaining in the hands of individuals after payment of direct taxes, in 1962 was about three and a third times its depression low. This difference reflects the fact that government costs and revenues—and taxes—have risen much faster and higher than the economy as a whole.

Corporate Profits after Taxes

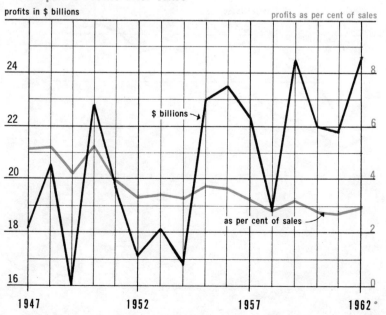

FAMILY FINANCES

average per family in 1960 prices . . .

income . . .

year	before taxes	after taxes	expenditures	installment credit outstanding	savings
1929	$4,174	$4,144	$3,922	$175	$208
1941	n.a.	n.a.	4,114	306	556
1942	n.a.	n.a.	n.a.	n.a.	n.a.
1943	n.a.	n.a.	n.a.	n.a.	n.a.
1944	n.a.	n.a.	4,315	86	1,455
1945	n.a.	n.a.	n.a.	n.a.	n.a.
1946	n.a.	n.a.	4,896	139	448
1947	5,352	4,822	4,823	195	139
1948	5,332	4,920	4,749	240	292
1949	5,156	4,782	4,715	302	218
1950	5,421	4,969	4,881	368	317
1951	5,617	5,057	4,861	354	410
1952	5,745	5,126	4,920	434	422
1953	5,980	5,332	5,123	507	440
1954	5,882	5,322	5,119	507	406
1955	6,167	5,568	5,397	607	370
1956	6,462	5,813	5,515	648	470
1957	6,520	5,863	5,571	662	463
1958	6,442	5,813	5,507	632	467
1959	6,687	6,010	5,756	720	432
1960	6,805	6,118	5,856	763	373
1961	6,854	6,157	5,848	753	442
1962	7,011	6,285	5,980	806	439

Average family income (in terms of 1960 purchasing power) in 1962 was 68 per cent above that of 1929, also a year of prosperity. Because of the sharp rise in direct taxes, however, the income remaining after payment of taxes increased by little more than 50 per cent. Average family expenditures also increased a little more than 50 per cent.

American families appear to be better borrowers than savers, for installment credit (in equivalent purchasing power) in 1962 was nearly five times the amount outstanding in 1929, but savings were little more than twice as large.

Average Family Income

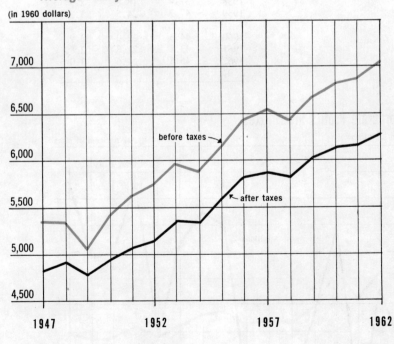

138

PERSONAL CONSUMPTION EXPENDITURES

percentage distribution . . .

		by type of product or service . . .			by purpose or use . . .											
year	total, billions	total	durable goods	non-durable goods	services	total	food, liquor, tobacco	clothing, personal care	housing	household operation	personal business	health, medical care	domestic transpor-tation	recreation	education	religion and welfare	foreign travel
1929	$79	100.0	11.6	47.8	40.6	100.0	28.7	14.9	17.9	9.8	7.0	3.6	9.4	4.8	1.4	1.5	1.0
1930	71	100.0	10.1	47.9	42.0	100.0	29.0	14.5	19.4	9.3	6.3	3.9	8.5	4.9	1.5	1.7	1.0
1931	61	100.0	9.0	47.1	43.9	100.0	28.0	14.4	20.9	9.2	6.3	4.1	8.0	4.6	1.7	1.8	1.0
1932	49	100.0	7.3	46.3	46.4	100.0	27.1	13.5	23.1	8.6	6.8	4.2	7.9	4.2	1.8	1.9	0.9
1933	46	100.0	7.5	48.0	44.5	100.0	27.5	12.9	22.5	8.7	7.1	4.3	8.6	4.0	1.7	1.9	0.8
1934	52	100.0	8.1	51.4	40.5	100.0	29.9	13.9	19.9	8.9	6.4	4.2	8.9	4.0	1.6	1.7	0.6
1935	56	100.0	9.1	52.0	38.9	100.0	31.3	13.7	18.5	9.0	6.3	4.1	9.4	4.0	1.6	1.5	0.6
1936	63	100.0	10.1	52.4	37.5	100.0	31.9	13.4	17.4	9.6	6.1	4.0	9.8	4.2	1.5	1.4	0.7
1937	67	100.0	10.3	52.4	37.3	100.0	32.0	13.2	17.1	9.9	6.2	4.0	9.7	4.4	1.5	1.3	0.7
1938	65	100.0	8.8	52.5	38.7	100.0	31.8	13.6	18.2	9.4	6.1	4.2	8.7	4.4	1.6	1.4	0.6
1939	68	100.0	9.9	51.9	38.2	100.0	31.0	13.7	18.0	9.8	6.0	4.2	9.4	4.4	1.6	1.4	0.5
1940	72	100.0	10.8	51.8	37.4	100.0	30.9	13.5	17.7	10.1	5.8	4.2	9.9	4.6	1.6	1.4	0.3
1941	82	100.0	11.8	52.8	35.4	100.0	31.5	14.0	16.6	10.5	5.4	4.0	10.3	4.6	1.5	1.3	0.3
1942	90	100.0	7.8	57.1	35.1	100.0	34.7	15.8	16.4	10.1	4.8	4.2	6.2	4.6	1.5	1.3	0.4
1943	100	100.0	6.6	58.9	34.5	100.0	36.2	17.3	15.3	9.2	4.5	4.2	5.5	4.2	1.6	1.4	0.6
1944	110	100.0	6.2	59.5	34.3	100.0	36.5	17.4	14.7	9.2	4.4	4.3	5.3	4.2	1.6	1.5	0.9
1945	122	100.0	6.7	60.1	33.2	100.0	36.6	17.6	13.9	9.3	4.2	4.2	5.6	4.4	1.5	1.4	1.3
1946	147	100.0	10.8	57.7	31.5	100.0	35.7	16.3	12.7	10.5	3.9	4.2	8.2	5.2	1.5	1.3	0.5
1947	165	100.0	12.5	56.4	31.1	100.0	35.2	15.0	12.9	11.3	4.0	4.1	9.3	5.0	1.5	1.2	0.5
1948	178	100.0	12.7	55.4	31.9	100.0	33.8	14.7	13.5	11.3	4.2	4.4	10.0	4.9	1.5	1.2	0.5
1949	181	100.0	13.6	53.3	33.1	100.0	32.3	14.0	14.1	10.9	4.4	4.5	11.5	4.9	1.6	1.2	0.6
1950	195	100.0	15.6	51.1	33.3	100.0	30.6	13.2	14.5	11.5	4.6	4.5	12.6	5.1	1.6	1.2	0.6
1951	210	100.0	14.1	52.4	33.5	100.0	31.6	13.2	14.7	11.3	4.7	4.5	11.7	4.9	1.6	1.2	0.6
1952	220	100.0	13.2	52.4	34.4	100.0	31.6	13.1	15.1	10.7	4.9	4.6	11.5	4.9	1.6	1.2	0.8
1953	233	100.0	14.1	50.7	35.2	100.0	30.3	12.6	15.4	10.5	5.1	4.8	12.7	4.9	1.6	1.2	0.9
1954	238	100.0	13.6	50.1	36.3	100.0	30.0	12.4	16.0	10.2	5.4	5.0	12.3	4.9	1.6	1.3	0.9
1955	257	100.0	15.4	48.6	36.0	100.0	28.9	12.2	15.7	10.6	5.5	5.0	13.8	4.9	1.6	1.2	0.9
1956	270	100.0	14.3	48.7	37.0	100.0	28.5	12.2	15.9	10.8	5.9	5.2	12.6	5.0	1.7	1.3	0.9
1957	285	100.0	14.2	48.2	37.6	100.0	28.2	12.0	16.2	10.4	6.0	5.4	12.8	5.0	1.8	1.3	0.9
1958	293	100.0	12.7	48.3	39.0	100.0	28.3	12.0	16.7	10.3	6.3	5.7	11.4	5.1	1.9	1.4	0.9
1959	314	100.0	13.9	46.9	39.2	100.0	27.0	12.0	16.5	10.4	6.5	5.8	12.5	5.1	2.0	1.3	0.9
1960	328	100.0	13.6	46.2	40.2	100.0	26.4	11.9	16.6	10.3	6.7	5.9	12.6	5.2	2.1	1.5	0.8
1961	338	100.0	12.9	46.0	41.1	100.0	26.3	11.8	17.1	10.2	6.8	6.2	11.8	5.4	2.1	1.5	0.8
1962	357	100.0	13.3	45.4	41.3	100.0	25.9	11.7	17.1	10.1	6.7	6.2	12.4	5.4	2.2	1.4	0.9

Since 1954, consumer spending for nondurable goods has fallen to less than half the total of all personal consumption expenditures. During the later depression years and in the war and postwar period the proportion was considerably higher.

Durable goods, such as automobiles, on the other hand, take a much larger share of the consumer's dollar at the present time than at the depth of the depression, when incomes were low, or during the war years, when such goods were in short supply.

Providing food and shelter for the family and running the household requires more than half of consumer expenditures. Another quarter is absorbed by costs of clothing, personal care and transportation.

Over the years, money spent for food and tobacco and for clothing and personal care has accounted for a declining share of total consumption expenditures. Health and medical care, transportation, recreation, and education have all increased in relative importance in their demands on the family purse.

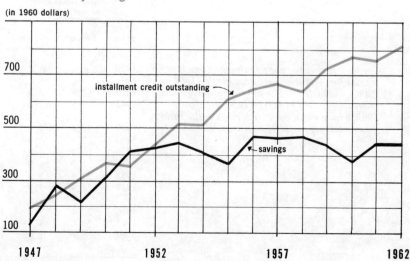

Growth of Installment Credit per Family and Family Savings

(in 1960 dollars)

installment credit outstanding

savings

1947　　　1952　　　1957　　　1962

700

500

300

100

FOOD, LIQUOR, AND TOBACCO CONSUMPTION

Per capita food consumption, measured in pounds and calories, has declined over the past three decades. But food expenditures have risen considerably, chiefly because of higher prices, but also because quality of diets has improved —with more protein and fewer carbohydrates. Many more foods are precooked and packaged, adding to their cost.

Frozen foods have become much more important in the American diet since World War II, consumption having increased from less than 11 pounds per capita in 1947 to more than 64 pounds in 1961.

| year | per capita expenditures for ... | | | per capita food consumption ... | | frozen foods available for consumption, pounds ... | |
	food	liquor	tobacco products	calories per day	pounds	total, millions	per capita
1929	$160	$16	$14	3,500	1,572	n.a.	n.a.
1930	146	13	12	3,480	1,537	n.a.	n.a.
1931	119	10	12	3,420	1,547	n.a.	n.a.
1932	91	7	11	3,360	1,509	n.a.	n.a.
1933	86	5	10	3,320	1,491	n.a.	n.a.
1934	96	16	11	3,280	1,492	n.a.	n.a.
1935	107	20	11	3,230	1,505	n.a.	n.a.
1936	119	25	12	3,320	1,511	n.a.	n.a.
1937	127	27	13	3,280	1,520	n.a.	n.a.
1938	120	25	13	3,290	1,519	n.a.	n.a.
1939	120	26	13	3,380	1,549	n.a.	n.a.
1940	126	27	14	3,370	1,548	n.a.	n.a.
1941	145	31	16	3,430	1,571	n.a.	n.a.
1942	175	38	18	3,370	1,566	n.a.	n.a.
1943	203	43	20	3,400	1,587	n.a.	n.a.
1944	221	49	20	3,390	1,640	n.a.	n.a.
1945	243	53	21	3,330	1,650	n.a.	n.a.
1946	287	59	25	3,350	1,646	n.a.	n.a.
1947	316	60	27	3,300	1,593	1,533	10.6
1948	327	54	28	3,240	1,527	1,793	12.2
1949	310	51	29	3,220	1,517	2,380	15.9
1950	312	51	29	3,290	1,502	3,317	21.8
1951	345	52	31	3,190	1,495	4,349	28.2
1952	354	54	33	3,230	1,491	5,449	34.8
1953	354	54	33	3,200	1,494	6,300	39.6
1954	354	52	32	3,180	1,485	7,249	44.8
1955	357	52	32	3,200	1,491	7,882	47.7
1956	369	53	33	3,200	1,496	9,008	53.6
1957	379	53	35	3,150	1,476	9,044	52.8
1958	385	53	37	3,160	1,463	8,768	50.4
1959	383	54	39	3,210	1,469	10,526	59.4
1960	386	54	40	3,180	1,467	11,019	61.2
1961	386	56	41	3,180	1,455	11,760	64.3
1962	394	57	42	3,170	n.a.	n.a.	n.a.

HEALTH AND MEDICAL CARE

Consumers spent about five times as much per capita for health and medical care in 1962 as they did in 1930. The number of physicians increased from 154,000 in 1930 to 260,000 in 1961, with a consequent reduction in the ratio of inhabitants per physician from 797 to 707.

| year | expenditures for ... total, public and private ... | | consumer, per capita | number of physicians, thousands | inhabitants per physician | number of hospital beds, thousands | inhabitants per hospital bed | number of persons covered by medical insurance ... | |
	billions	per cent of GNP						millions	per thousand inhabitants
1930	n.a.	n.a.	$23	154	797	956	128	n.a.	n.a.
1935	n.a.	n.a.	18	163	782	1,075	119	n.a.	n.a.
1940	$3.9	4.1	23	175	757	1,226	108	3.0	23
1945	7.5	3.5	36	n.a.	n.a.	1,739	77	4.7	37
1950	12.4	4.7	58	203	749	1,456	104	21.6	144
1955	17.7	4.7	77	218	761	1,604	102	55.5	342
1956	19.2	4.7	84	222	762	1,608	104	64.9	392
1957	21.0	4.9	90	227	759	1,559	109	71.8	426
1958	22.8	5.2	95	231	758	1,578	110	75.4	438
1959	24.9	5.3	102	237	751	1,613	110	82.6	471
1960	26.9	5.4	108	256	706	1,658	109	87.5	491
1961	29.0	5.7	113	260	707	1,670	110	94.2	520
1962	n.a.	n.a.	118	n.a.	n.a.	n.a.	n.a.	98.2	530

HOUSING AND HOUSEHOLD OPERATION

year	expenditures for private nonfarm residential construction . . . total, millions	per cent of GNP	consumption expenditures, billions housing	household operation	nonfarm dwelling units started, thousands	nonfarm homeowners' mortgage debt, billions
1929	$3,625	3.5	$14.5	$13.5	509	$18.9
1930	2,075	2.3	14.1	11.2	330	18.9
1931	1,565	2.1	13.1	9.6	254	18.1
1932	630	1.1	11.6	7.6	134	16.7
1933	470	0.8	10.4	7.2	93	15.4
1934	625	1.0	10.3	7.8	126	15.6
1935	1,010	1.4	10.4	8.5	221	15.4
1936	1,565	1.9	10.9	9.7	319	15.4
1937	1,875	2.1	11.5	10.6	336	15.5
1938	1,990	2.3	11.8	9.7	406	15.8
1939	2,680	2.9	12.1	10.4	515	16.3
1940	2,985	3.0	12.7	11.1	603	17.4
1941	3,510	2.8	13.6	12.7	706	18.4
1942	1,715	1.1	14.7	13.0	356	18.2
1943	885	0.5	15.4	13.3	191	17.8
1944	815	0.4	16.1	14.4	142	17.9
1945	1,276	0.6	16.9	16.0	209	18.6
1946	4,752	2.3	18.7	20.9	670	23.0
1947	7,535	3.2	21.2	24.7	849	28.2
1948	10,122	3.9	24.0	27.1	932	33.3
1949	9,642	3.7	25.6	27.2	1,025	37.6
1950	14,100	5.0	28.2	30.8	1,396	45.2
1951	12,529	3.8	30.8	33.0	1,091	51.7
1952	12,842	3.7	33.3	33.5	1,127	58.5
1953	13,777	3.8	35.8	35.6	1,104	66.1
1954	15,379	4.2	38.0	36.4	1,220	75.7
1955	18,705	4.7	40.4	40.8	1,329	88.2
1956	17,677	4.2	43.0	44.1	1,118	99.0
1957	17,019	3.8	46.1	46.1	1,042	107.6
1958	18,047	4.1	49.0	47.9	1,209	117.7
1959	24,962	5.2	51.7	51.9	1,531	130.9
1960	22,546	4.5	54.6	54.5	1,274	141.3
1961	22,499	4.3	57.4	56.3	1,337	153.0
1962	24,833	4.5	60.6	58.8	1,460	168.7

The number of nonfarm dwelling units erected in 1962 was almost three times the number in prosperous 1929, but expenditures for such construction were almost seven times as great.

Consumer expenditures for housing (including rent or mortgage and other costs for owner-occupied dwellings, utilities, and structural repairs) were more than four times as large in 1962 as in 1929. Household operating expenses (including household furniture, equipment, and supplies; household business, such as insurance and legal fees; telephone; household help; cleaning; repair and maintenance) were also more than four times those of 1929.

Mortgage debt owed by homeowners showed the most spectacular rise—from less than $19 billion in 1929 to almost $169 billion in 1962.

These changes reflect not only the rise in population and in the number of households since 1929 but also the fact that construction costs have risen more rapidly than the general price level, while mortgage credit has been extended more liberally.

HOUSING CHARACTERISTICS

	1950	1960
All dwelling units, thousands	46,137	58,326
In one unit detached, thousands	29,500	40,870
Average number of rooms per unit	4.6	4.9
Per cent with . . .		
running water	82.8	92.9
flush toilet, exclusive use	71.4	86.8
bathtub or shower, exclusive use	69.3	85.2
Per cent occupied	93.1	90.9
Occupied dwelling units, thousands	42,969	53,024
Average number of persons per unit	3.1	3.0
Per cent . . .		
owner-occupied	55.0	61.9
with 1 person per unit	9.3	13.3
with 2-5 persons per unit	79.6	75.2
with 6 or more persons per unit	11.1	11.5
with 1 or fewer persons per room	84.2	88.5
with more than 1 person per room	15.8	11.5
with radio	95.7	91.5
with TV	12.0	87.3
cooking with gas	59.5	63.7
electricity	15.0	30.8
other	25.5	5.5

The quality of American housing improved substantially during the 1950s, as reflected in the larger number of rooms per dwelling unit and the higher proportion of units with running water, flush toilets, bathtubs or showers, and gas or electric cookstoves in 1960 than in 1950.

A larger proportion of families owned their homes in 1960 than in 1950, and the average number of persons per dwelling unit and per room declined during the decade.

Although there was an actual decline in the proportion of homes with radios, from 96 per cent in 1950 to 92 per cent in 1960, TV sets were to be found in nearly 9 out of 10 dwellings in 1960, in contrast to little more than 1 out of 10 in 1950.

EDUCATION

year	enrollment, thousands ... elementary and secondary schools ...			higher institutions	number of teachers, thousands ... public elementary and secondary schools	higher institutions	number graduated annually ... from high school ...		from college ...		expenditures for public elementary and secondary schools ...	
	total	public	private				total, thousands	as per cent of population 17 years of age	total, thousands	as per cent of population 20-24 years of age	total, millions	operating cost per pupil
1900	16,855	15,503	1,352	238	423	24	95	6.4	27	0.4	$215	$17
1910	19,372	17,814	1,558	355	523	36	156	8.8	37	0.4	426	28
1920	23,277	21,578	1,699	598	680	49	311	16.8	49	0.5	1,036	54
1930	28,329	25,678	2,651	1,101	854	82	667	29.0	122	1.1	2,317	87
1936	29,006	26,367	2,639	1,208	871	121	1,015	n.a.	143	1.3	1,969	74
1940	28,045	25,434	2,611	1,494	875	147	1,221	50.8	186	1.6	2,344	88
1946	26,124	23,300	2,824	1,677	831	165	1,080	47.9	136	1.2	2,907	136
1950	28,491	25,111	3,380	2,659	914	247	1,200	59.0	432	3.8	5,838	209
1952	30,372	26,563	3,809	2,302	963	244	1,196	58.6	330	3.1	7,344	244
1954	33,175	28,836	4,339	2,515	1,032	266	1,276	60.0	291	2.9	9,092	265
1956	35,872	31,163	4,709	2,637	1,133	299	1,415	62.3	309	2.7	10,955	294
1958	38,952	33,695	5,257	2,900	1,238	345	1,506	64.8	363	3.3	13,569	341
1960	41,762	36,087	5,675	3,236	1,355	381	1,860	65.0	392	3.6	15,613	375
1970	50,766	n.a.	n.a.	5,565	—	—	—	—	—	—	—	—
1975	53,916	n.a.	n.a.	6,506	—	—	—	—	—	—	—	—

The population growth during the present century has brought a steady rise in total enrollment and in numbers of teachers at all school levels, but the largest percentage increases have occured in high schools and colleges.

In 1960, the high school graduating class was nearly 20 times as large as in 1900. The number of students receiving college degrees was more than 14 times as large. Nearly two thirds of all young people between 17 and 18 years old have high school diplomas, but less than 4 per cent of the 20-to-24-year-olds have graduated from college.

Because of the expansion of teaching staffs and educational facilities and the rising salaries and other costs, expenditures for education have risen much more rapidly than has the number of pupils and teachers. This is reflected in the fact that operating costs per pupil in public elementary and secondary schools averaged $375 in 1960—22 times the amount spent in 1900.

At the end of World War II there were only about 10 per cent more cars on American streets and highways than there had been 15 years earlier. Since 1945, however, some 40 million cars have been added to the total number registered, and there are now nearly 3 times as many cars in use as in 1929.

Road-building has more than kept pace with automobile ownership—there are now about four times as many miles of hard-surfaced streets and roads as in 1929.

Consumer spending for travel and transportation, including foreign travel, has risen steeply over the past 30 years, reflecting the rise in automobile use and a tremendous increase in air travel. The railroads, however, are carrying less than half as many passengers today as in 1929.

TRANSPORTATION AND TRAVEL

year	automobiles ... registrations, millions	consumption expenditures for ... amount, billions	per cent of all consumption expenditures	miles of roads and highways, thousands ... total	surfaced	travel by railroad and airline ... passengers, millions rail	air	passenger-miles, billions rail	air	foreign travel expenditures millions
1929	23.1	$2.6	3.2	3,024	662	786.4	0.2	31.2	n.a.	$511
1932	20.8	0.6	1.3	3,040	879	480.7	0.5	17.0	0.1	285
1933	20.6	0.8	1.7	3,029	914	434.8	0.5	16.4	0.2	206
1934	21.5	1.0	2.0	3,050	992	452.2	0.5	18.1	0.2	207
1935	22.5	1.5	2.7	3,050	1,080	448.1	0.7	18.5	0.3	217
1938	25.2	1.2	1.9	2,992	1,276	454.5	1.1	21.7	0.5	262
1939	26.1	1.7	2.5	3,007	1,318	454.0	1.6	22.7	0.7	209
1940	27.4	2.2	3.1	3,017	1,367	456.1	2.5	23.8	1.1	94
1941	29.5	2.7	3.3	3,309	1,607	488.7	3.5	29.4	1.4	172
1942	27.9	0.4	0.5	3,309	1,630	672.4	3.1	53.7	1.4	257
1943	25.9	0.4	0.4	3,311	1,646	887.7	3.0	87.9	1.6	420
1944	25.5	0.3	0.3	3,311	1,655	915.8	4.0	95.7	2.2	828
1945	25.7	0.4	0.3	3,319	1,721	897.4	6.6	91.8	3.4	1,458
1946	28.1	2.4	1.7	3,316	1,730	794.8	12.2	64.8	5.9	536
1947	30.7	4.6	2.8	3,326	1,785	706.6	12.9	46.0	6.1	668
1948	33.2	5.7	3.2	3,323	1,815	645.5	13.2	41.2	6.0	774
1949	36.3	8.1	4.5	3,322	1,865	556.7	15.1	35.1	6.8	938
1950	40.3	10.7	5.5	3,313	1,939	488.0	17.3	31.8	8.0	906
1951	42.5	9.4	4.5	3,326	1,998	485.5	22.7	34.7	10.6	1,110
1952	43.8	8.9	4.0	3,343	2,070	471.0	25.0	34.0	12.5	1,444
1953	46.4	11.8	5.1	3,366	2,160	458.3	28.7	31.7	14.8	1,926
1954	48.5	11.3	4.8	3,395	2,228	440.8	32.3	29.3	16.8	1,970
1955	52.1	15.8	6.2	3,418	2,273	433.3	38.2	28.5	19.9	2,069
1956	54.2	13.4	5.0	3,430	2,323	430.0	41.7	28.2	22.4	2,216
1957	55.9	14.6	5.1	3,453	2,367	413.0	48.5	25.9	25.3	2,268
1958	56.9	11.5	3.9	3,479	2,446	382.0	48.1	23.3	25.3	2,387
1959	59.6	15.3	4.9	3,511	2,500	354.0	55.0	22.4	29.3	2,542
1960	61.7	15.9	4.8	3,546	2,557	327.0	56.4	21.6	30.6	2,682
1961	63.3	14.3	4.2	3,573	2,625	318.0	56.9	20.5	31.1	2,652
1962	65.6	17.3	4.9	n.a.	n.a.	313.2	60.4	20.1	33.6	3,068

Expenditures at all levels of government—federal, state, and local—have risen steeply since 1929, although they dipped slightly in the early years of the long depression and dipped again for several years after the World War II peak in 1944. Total government expenditures in 1962 amounted to a net of $161 billion, compared with $103 billion in 1944 and less than $11 billion in 1929, 1932, and 1933.

Although tax revenues at all government levels have also climbed steadily, they have failed to keep pace with the rise in expenditures. The federal debt in 1962 was more than 15 times as large as it was in 1929, reflecting the fact that in 23 of the succeeding 33 years the federal government operated at a deficit.

The federal surplus or deficit shown here is that shown in the National Income Accounts by the U. S. Department of Commerce, which differs from the federal administrative budget's surplus or deficit in certain technical details. Examples of the differences are shown in the figures below for the fiscal and calendar year 1962 (in billions):

	calendar year	fiscal year
Federal budget	$ −7.2	$ −6.4
National Income Account	−4.3	−2.7

	expenditures ...					tax revenue ... millions ...					
	total, excluding intergovernmental transfers, billions	federal ... total, millions	national defense ... amount, millions	as per cent of total	state and local, millions	total	federal	state and local	total, per capita	federal surplus or deficit, billions	federal debt, billions
year											
1929	$10.2	$2,645	$715	27.0	$7,699	$10,033	$3,600	$6,433	$82	$1.2	$16.5
1930	11.0	2,766	733	26.5	8,381	9,508	2,838	6,670	77	0.3	16.5
1931	12.3	4,183	718	17.2	8,448	8,272	1,855	6,417	67	−2.1	18.5
1932	10.6	3,188	675	21.2	7,553	7,977	1,813	6,164	64	−1.5	21.3
1933	10.7	3,986	594	14.9	7,192	8,255	2,503	5,752	66	−1.3	24.3
1934	12.8	6,394	625	9.8	8,069	8,854	2,942	5,912	70	−2.9	30.4
1935	13.3	6,527	812	12.4	8,519	10,237	3,775	6,462	80	−2.6	34.4
1936	15.9	8,501	926	10.9	8,105	10,583	3,882	6,701	83	−3.5	37.7
1937	14.8	7,225	984	13.6	8,366	12,758	5,403	7,355	99	−0.2	39.2
1938	16.6	8,451	1,053	12.5	8,916	12,949	5,344	7,605	100	−2.0	40.5
1939	17.5	8,955	1,287	12.9	9,555	12,425	4,783	7,642	95	−2.2	42.6
1940	18.5	10,089	3,767	37.3	9,235	12,688	4,878	7,810	96	−1.4	44.8
1941	28.8	20,539	14,987	73.0	9,021	21,342	12,840	8,502	160	−5.1	56.3
1942	64.0	56,141	43,548	77.6	8,779	20,793	12,265	8,528	154	−33.2	101.7
1943	93.4	85,972	69,928	81.3	8,369	43,657	34,886	8,771	323	−46.7	154.4
1944	103.1	95,585	78,956	82.6	8,434	49,095	40,321	8,774	367	−54.6	211.9
1945	92.9	84,826	62,196	73.3	8,987	45,855	36,407	9,448	344	−42.3	252.7
1946	47.0	37,014	28,772	77.7	11,098	46,380	36,286	10,094	330	2.2	229.7
1947	43.8	31,135	13,069	42.0	14,414	50,049	37,946	12,103	347	12.2	223.3
1948	51.0	35,414	12,340	34.8	17,567	51,218	37,876	13,342	349	8.0	216.5
1949	59.5	41,599	12,958	31.1	20,156	48,795	33,780	15,015	327	−2.5	218.6
1950	61.1	41,027	17,727	43.2	22,428	51,100	35,186	15,914	337	9.2	218.7
1951	79.4	58,045	33,210	57.2	23,790	75,094	56,967	18,127	488	6.4	218.5
1952	94.4	71,613	47,452	66.3	25,447	79,066	59,744	19,323	503	−3.9	222.9
1953	102.0	77,715	47,330	60.9	27,136	83,704	62,796	20,908	527	−7.4	228.1
1954	96.7	69,570	42,113	60.5	30,053	84,476	62,409	22,067	522	−5.8	230.2
1955	98.6	68,915	40,046	58.1	32,713	81,072	57,589	23,483	491	3.8	231.5
1956	104.3	71,844	41,332	57.5	35,715	91,593	65,226	26,368	548	5.7	225.4
1957	115.3	79,721	45,407	57.0	39,638	98,632	69,815	28,817	579	2.0	224.4
1958	126.6	87,921	45,884	52.2	44,108	98,387	68,007	30,380	568	−9.4	232.7
1959	131.6	91,417	47,440	51.9	46,957	99,636	67,257	32,379	564	−1.1	243.2
1960	136.8	93,064	47,073	50.6	49,984	113,120	77,003	36,117	628	3.5	241.0
1961	149.3	102,750	50,647	49.3	54,393	116,331	77,470	38,861	636	−4.5	248.1
1962	161.0	109,752	55,200	50.3	58,655	126,725	83,822	42,903	682	−4.3	255.9

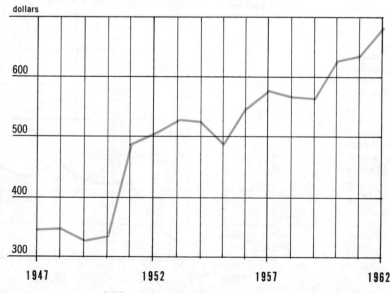

Rise in Tax Load per Capita

dollars

600

500

400

300

1947   1952   1957   1962

PUBLIC WELFARE

	cash benefits to individuals, billions ...				civilian ...		social insurance ...	old-age retirement ...		unemployment ...		total expenditures for veterans' welfare and medical programs, millions
year	total	federal including military	state and local	military	amount	per cent of total government expenditures	total contributions, millions	amount of benefits, millions	beneficiaries, thousands	amount of benefits, millions	beneficiaries, thousands	
1929	$0.9	$0.7	$0.2	$0.4	$0.5	4.9	$ 243	—	—	—	—	n.a.
1930	1.0	0.7	0.3	0.5	0.5	4.5	253	—	—	—	—	n.a.
1931	2.0	1.7	0.3	0.5	1.5	12.1	262	—	—	—	—	n.a.
1932	1.4	0.9	0.5	0.6	0.8	7.5	278	—	—	—	—	n.a.
1933	1.5	0.7	0.8	0.5	1.0	9.3	285	—	—	—	—	n.a.
1934	1.6	0.6	1.0	0.4	1.2	9.4	304	—	—	—	—	n.a.
1935	1.8	0.6	1.2	0.4	1.4	10.5	333	—	—	—	—	$450
1936	3.0	2.1	0.9	0.4	2.6	16.4	598	—	—	—	—	480
1937	1.8	0.8	1.0	0.4	1.4	9.5	1,800	—	—	—	—	485
1938	2.4	1.2	1.2	0.4	2.0	12.0	1,977	—	—	—	—	494
1939	2.5	1.2	1.3	0.5	2.0	11.4	2,136	—	—	—	—	513
1940	2.7	1.4	1.3	0.5	2.2	11.9	2,282	$17	77	$535	1,024	535
1941	2.6	1.4	1.2	0.5	2.1	7.3	2,784	55	272	359	545	535
1942	2.6	1.4	1.2	0.5	2.1	3.3	3,468	80	323	350	554	538
1943	2.4	1.2	1.2	0.5	1.9	2.0	4,516	97	386	81	117	556
1944	3.0	1.8	1.2	0.9	2.1	2.0	5,173	119	463	67	91	623
1945	5.6	4.3	1.3	2.4	2.1	2.3	6,138	157	592	575	569	890
1946	10.9	9.2	1.7	3.8	7 1	15.1	5,981	222	843	2,878	2,794	3,014
1947	11.1	8.9	2.2	3.8	7.3	16.7	5,683	288	1,068	1,786	1,847	6,689
1948	10.6	7.7	2.9	2.7	7.9	15.5	5,220	352	1,295	1,332	1,373	6,880
1949	11.6	8.7	2.9	2.6	9.0	15.1	5,737	437	1,575	2,272	2,214	7,009
1950	14.3	10.9	3.4	2.6	11.7	19.1	6,870	651	1,918	1,468	1,414	6,381
1951	11.6	8.7	2.9	2.6	9.0	11.3	8,170	1,321	2,757	863	1,416	5,506
1952	12.0	8.9	3.1	3.0	9.0	9.5	8,614	1,539	3,187	1,044	932	4,720
1953	12.9	9.7	3.2	3.1	9.8	9.6	8,728	2,175	3,889	1,051	886	4,221
1954	15.0	11.6	3.4	3.2	11.8	12.2	9,695	2,698	4,590	2,292	1,814	4,115
1955	16.0	12.5	3.5	3.4	12.6	12.8	10,995	3,748	5,443	1,560	1,235	4,369
1956	17.2	13.5	3.7	3.4	13.8	13.2	12,586	4,361	6,191	1,541	1,135	4,619
1957	20.1	16.0	4.1	3.5	16.6	14.4	14,522	5,688	7,623	1,913	1,354	4,691
1958	24.5	20.0	4.5	3.8	20.7	16.4	14,835	6,477	8,738	4,210	2,969	5,006
1959	25.4	20.6	4.8	3.9	21.5	16.3	17,574	7,607	9,631	2,805	2,856	5,094
1960	27.3	22.2	5.1	4.1	23.2	17.0	20,571	8,196	10,310	3,025	1,795	5,091
1961	31.3	25.9	5.4	4.4	26.9	18.0	21,439	9,032	11,128	4,358	2,555	5,278
1962	32.5	26.7	5.8	4.6	27.9	17.3	23,900	10,162	12,248	3,145	1,794	5,400

Transfer payments to persons for public welfare in 1962 were 36 times as large, and social insurance contributions almost 100 times as large, as in 1929. Contributions were ten times as large in 1962 as in 1940, when benefit payments under the federal old-age retirement first became numerically significant. (Social insurance contributions prior to 1937 were mainly to federal, state, and local employee retirement programs.)

The number of beneficiaries and total amount of benefits under federal old-age retirement laws have also been rising astronomically. In 1962 more than 12 million persons received benefits in excess of $10 billion.

Rise in Public Welfare — Cash Benefits to Individual

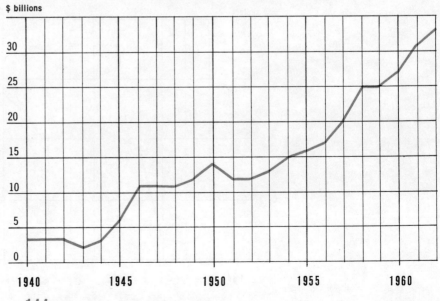

LAND USE
millions of acres

year	total, (excluding Hawaii and Alaska)	cropland	pasture and grazing land	forest and woodland not grazed	other
1900	1,903	319	1,131	278	175
1910	1,903	347	1,121	255	180
1920	1,903	402	1,066	251	184
1930	1,903	413	1,042	273	175
1940	1,905	399	1,065	260	181
1950	1,904	409	1,020	286	189
1959	1,902	392	939	371	200

The total acreage of land in the United States varies slightly over a period of time because of river and ocean erosion and land reclamation and because of corrections in measurement.

Although about 70 per cent of all land in the 48 contiguous states of the United States is used for broadly defined agricultural purposes (for growing crops and for pasture), the 1959 proportion was smaller than in earlier years.

FARMING

year	farm population... total, millions	farm population... as per cent of total population	farm employment, millions	average number of persons each farm worker supplies	index of productivity per man-hour (1947-1949 =100)	number of farms, thousands	value of farm production, millions	net income per farm... current prices	net income per farm... 1960 prices
1900	n.a.	n.a.	12.8	6.95	n.a.	5,737	$3,991	n.a.	n.a.
1910	32.1	34.7	13.6	7.07	45	6,406	5,780	n.a.	n.a.
1920	32.0	30.1	13.4	8.27	49	6,518	12,600	$1,190	$1,503
1930	30.5	24.9	12.5	9.75	53	6,546	9,055	650	1,313
1940	30.5	23.2	11.0	10.69	67	6,350	8,382	720	1,731
1950	23.0	15.3	9.9	14.56	112	5,648	28,512	2,479	2,912
1955	19.1	11.6	8.4	19.29	149	4,654	29,556	2,529	2,717
1960	15.6	8.7	7.1	26.34	206	3,949	34,012	3,044	3,044
1961	14.8	8.1	6.9	27.43	210	3,811	34,886	3,359	3,326
1962	14.3	7.7	6.7	28.50	217	3,688	35,921	3,602	3,532

The substantial increase in American agricultural output since 1910 in the face of a steady decline in the number of farm workers reflects a great rise in productivity. (Farm employment data shown in this table are Department of Agriculture estimates, which differ somewhat from the Department of Labor figures discussed in Chapters 3 and 19.)

Output per man-hour is today almost five times that of 1910, and the average farm worker now produces enough to supply four times as many consumers as in that year. These gains have been made possible by the growing size of farms and the increasing use of tractors and other mechanical aids to production and the widening use of fertilizers and pesticides.

ENERGY PRODUCTION

year	primary energy, millions of tons, coal equivalent ... total	bituminous and lignite	anthracite	crude petroleum	natural gas	water power	total electric energy production, billions of K.W.H.
1900	301.3	212.3	55.6	14.1	9.7	9.5	6.0
1910	586.8	417.1	81.9	46.4	20.9	20.6	24.8
1920	815.5	568.7	86.9	98.1	33.7	28.2	56.6
1930	844.2	467.5	67.3	198.8	82.0	28.7	114.6
1940	957.6	460.8	49.9	299.6	113.7	33.6	179.9
1950	1,317.2	516.3	42.7	437.0	261.1	60.0	388.7
1960	1,597.1	415.5	18.2	570.0	527.6	65.8	841.6
1961	1,614.3	403.0	16.9	580.4	547.2	66.9	878.7
1962	1,678.6	423.0	16.3	592.4	572.9	73.9	943.1

Total energy production in 1962 was more than five times as large as in 1900. It rose steadily from 301 million tons coal equivalent in 1900 to 1.7 billion tons in 1962.

The total energy trend reflects differing movements of the various components. Production of both bituminous coal and anthracite is far below the peak of 1920, while output of petroleum, natural gas, and hydroelectric energy has moved steadily upward.

FOREIGN TRADE AND BALANCE OF PAYMENTS

Although merchandise imports and exports have fluctuated considerably from year to year, America's exports have generally exceeded imports since 1929. The result has been a positive, or "favorable," balance on merchandise trade, as well as on "invisible" trade, which includes travel, shipping, income from investments, and foreign insurance.

During recent years, however, this positive balance has been more than offset by foreign aid payments and by the continuing export of capital for foreign investment. The over-all balance of payments has therefore been negative in 12 of the 13 years since 1950, with a resultant loss of more than $8 billion in gold from American reserves.

Despite this outflow of gold, American investors have invested about $33 billion more in enterprises abroad than foreign investors have invested in U.S. industries and commercial ventures.

| year | merchandise trade, millions ... | | | balance on goods and services, millions | foreign aid (nonmilitary), millions | net investment position abroad, billions | gold flow, millions | balance of payments, millions |
| | exports ... | | | | | | | |
	total	agricultural	imports					
1929	$5,347	$1,693	$4,463	$1,148	n.a.	n.a.	$143	$−53
1930	3,929	1,201	3,104	1,032	n.a.	$8.8	310	598
1931	2,494	821	2,120	516	n.a.	12.1	−133	1,132
1932	1,667	662	1,343	407	n.a.	n.a.	53	−726
1933	1,736	694	1,510	358	n.a.	n.a.	−131	323
1934	2,238	733	1,763	601	n.a.	n.a.	1,266	1,140
1935	2,404	747	2,462	128	n.a.	7.1	1,822	1,174
1936	2,590	709	2,546	115	n.a.	n.a.	1,272	896
1937	3,451	797	3,181	297	n.a.	n.a.	1,364	1,053
1938	3,243	828	2,173	1,291	n.a.	n.a.	1,799	1,482
1939	3,347	655	2,409	1,066		1.8	3,174	1,915
1940	4,124	517	2,698	1,719	n.a.	−1.3	4,243	2,890
1941	5,343	669	3,416	2,410	n.a.		719	1,119
1942	9,187	1,179	3,499	6,413	n.a.	n.a.	−23	−205
1943	15,115	2,074	4,599	11,038	n.a.	n.a.	−757	−1,979
1944	16,969	2,096	5,043	12,452	n.a.	n.a.	−1,350	−1,859
1945	12,473	2,254	5,245	6,041	n.a.	−0.8	−548	−2,737
1946	11,707	3,173	5,073	7,744	$5,293	12.8	623	1,261
1947	16,015	3,957	6,979	11,529	6,121	10.9	2,162	4,567
1948	13,193	3,472	7,563	6,440	4,918	12.9	1,530	1,005
1949	12,149	3,578	6,879	6,149	5,649	13.8	164	175
1950	10,117	2,873	9,108	1,779	3,640	13.3	−1,743	−3,580
1951	14,123	4,040	11,202	3,671	3,191	14.0	53	−305
1952	13,319	3,431	10,838	2,226	2,380	14.2	379	−1,046
1953	12,281	2,848	10,990	386	2,055	15.4	−1,161	−2,152
1954	12,799	3,054	10,354	1,828	1,554	14.8	−298	−1,550
1955	14,280	3,198	11,527	2,009	2,211	15.4	−41	−1,145
1956	17,379	4,170	12,804	3,967	2,362	17.3	306	−935
1957	19,390	4,506	13,291	5,729	2,574	23.0	798	520
1958	16,264	3,854	12,952	2,206	2,587	24.4	−2,275	−3,529
1959	16,282	3,955	15,310	134	1,986	22.7	−731	−3,743
1960	19,459	4,831	14,723	3,769	2,769	26.8	−1,702	−3,881
1961	19,913	5,029	14,497	5,444	2,782	27.3	−742	−2,370
1962	20,479	5,031	16,145	4,826	2,998	32.8	−907	−2,186

Trade Balance on Goods and Services

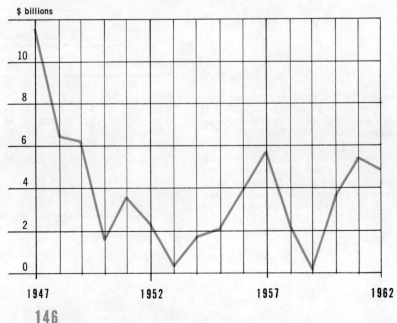

$ billions

| 1947 | 1952 | 1957 | 1962 |

Sources

The statistical base for this volume is the Twentieth Century Fund publication, *America's Needs and Resources, a New Survey,* by J. Frederic Dewhurst and Associates, published in 1955.

In bringing the statistics in the 1955 publication up to date, current issues of the same basic statistical publications were used, so the source notes to tables and footnotes to chapters in that volume generally still serve as guides to students who are seeking additional information.

Projections are based largely on the National Economic Projections Series, prepared by the Center for Economic Projections, National Planning Association, and on projections made by the U.S. Bureau of the Census.

The list below shows the most important of the source materials used. If various issues of publications issued at regular intervals were used, no dates are given, but in all cases the latest issues available as of December 1963 have been consulted.

Agriculture, U. S. Department of:
> *Agricultural Statistics,* annual.
> *Farm Income Situation.*

Board of Governors of the Federal Reserve System:
> *Federal Reserve Bulletin,* monthly.

Commerce, U. S. Department of:
> Bureau of the Census:
>> *Business Cycle Developments,* monthly.
>> *Census of Business, 1958.*
>> *Census of Housing, 1960.*
>> *Census of Manufactures, 1958.*
>> *Census of Population, 1960,* Vol. I—*Characteristics of the Population.* Part A—*Number of Inhabitants;* and other reports.
>> *Construction Reports,* monthly series.
>> *Current Population Reports.*
>> *Governmental Finances in 1962,* annual.
>> *Historical Statistics of the United States, Colonial Times to 1957, A Statistical Abstract Supplement.*
>> *Statistical Abstract of the United States,* annual.

> Office of Business Economics:
>> *Balance of Payments Statistical Supplement, 1870-1961* (supplement to *Survey of Current Business,* 1963).
>> *Business Statistics.*
>> *National Income* (supplement to *Survey of Current Business*), 1954.
>> *Survey of Current Business,* monthly.
>> *United States Income and Output* (supplement to *Survey of Current Business*), 1958.

Executive Office of the President:
> Bureau of the Budget:
>> *The Budget of the United States Government,* annual.
> Council of Economic Advisers:
>> *Economic Indicators,* monthly.
>> *Economic Report of the President,* annual.

Health, Education, and Welfare, U.S. Department of:
  National Vital Statistics Division, U. S. Public Health Service:
    Vital Statistics of the United States, annual.
  Office of Education:
    Digest of Educational Statistics, 1963.
  Social Security Administration:
    Social Security Bulletin, monthly.
Labor, U. S. Department of:
  Bureau of Labor Statistics:
    Employment and Earnings, monthly with annual supplement.
    Monthly Labor Review and annual supplements.
    Monthly Report on the Labor Force.
Private publications:
    Aerospace Facts and Figures, annual, Aerospace Industries Association of America, Washington.
    Automobile Facts and Figures, annual, Automobile Manufacturers Association, Detroit.
    Motor Truck Facts, annual, Automobile Manufacturers Association, Detroit.

Symbols used in tabular material

n.a.   not available
0 or 0.0   nil or negligible
—   not applicable or, for 1970 and 1975, no projections made

This book may be kept